HAPPY HOMES

HAPPY HOMES

Cooperation, Community
and the Edinburgh Colonies

RICHARD RODGER

THE WORD BANK

© Richard Rodger 2022

Published by Word Bank 2022

Word Bank is a
communty publishing
collective run by
Edinburgh Old Town
Development Trust
Scottish Charity no. SCO42964

The author has asserted his moral rights.

British Library Cataloguing-in-Publication Data.

A catalogue record for this book is available from the
British Library.

ISBN 978 0 9930544 9 5

Design and typset by
derek.rodger21@outlook.com

Jacket design
Astrid Jaekel

Printed by
Bell & Bain Ltd, Glasgow

Contents

Preface	7
Happy Homes	11
1. Housing Quality and Environmental Inequality	13
2. Arrested Development	25
3. Verbal Battlegrounds	29
4. Re-thinking the City	35
5. A Change of Tone	55
6. Building Cooperation	59
7. Structural Strength	69
8. From Strength to Strength	79
9. Building Phases	99
10. War, Depression and Decline	123
11. Who Lived in the Colonies?	131
12. Legacies	151
Appendices	159
Notes	169
Bibliography	180
Acknowledgements	183
Index	185

PHOTO: John Reiach

Reid Terrace, Stockbridge, the first development undertaken by ECBC

Preface

REID TERRACE, Stockbridge, the first street in the first Colony development, has for 160 years always been a presence in my life and the life of three previous generations of my family. No social gathering would pass without reference to the street, the names of neighbours, where they moved. My great grandfather, my grandad, and my father lived there for almost a century.

It was through this oral history of Reid Terrace that my personal history was constructed. My great grandfather moved to an upper colony house in 1861; twenty years later, no. 40 housed eight (soon to be nine) Rodgers. In the 1880s, two boys emigrated to Rhodesia and settled near Bulawayo. For the girls, like many their age, the First World War intervened; they never married. These were the great aunts who provided scraps of information about family life in Edinburgh Colony houses which I absorbed all too casually.

Unpicking this folklore through historical sources reveals much. As plasterer and upholsterer the first two Rodger generations preserved the link to the building industry and the Edinburgh Cooperative Building Company Limited (ECBC). As owner occupiers, and therefore shareholders in the Company, they also bought in to the aspirational ethos of self-improvement. This might all seem to corroborate a positive impression of the Colonies – the 'received version'. But the account developed here in *Happy Homes* challenges that comfortable version of the ECBC in some important respects. Mostly Colony houses were not owner occupied – they were tenanted. Mostly skilled artisans (the 'labour aristocracy') and building workers were a minority in Colony houses. Women were one of the largest ownership categories, the majority of whom were widows and 'rentiers' – that is, with incomes largely obtained from 'unearned' income – rents, dividends, and interest.

The ECBC was itself preoccupied with dividends, and by retaining essentially the same house design from the 1880s failed to recognise the shifting nature of housing preferences in the twentieth century.

It paid the price. Outmoded, it struggled on after 1914, lacking the dynamism of its first manager, James Colville.

So *Happy Homes* makes three new contributions:

- it provides a deeper understanding of the mid-nineteenth century social, political, and religious forces that contributed to the formation in 1861 of the ECBC;

- it reveals the social, household, gender, birthplaces and occupational characteristics of each of the eleven colony developments; and

- it shows how soundly built, carefully designed properties could provide attractive, affordable accommodation for family life on what were in reality 'new housing estates' on the fringes of the city.

Perhaps in the twenty first century we have something to learn from the Edinburgh Cooperative Building Company Limited.

Richard Rodger
June 2022

Preface

**Edinburgh Cooperative Building Company
Location of Colonies Developments**

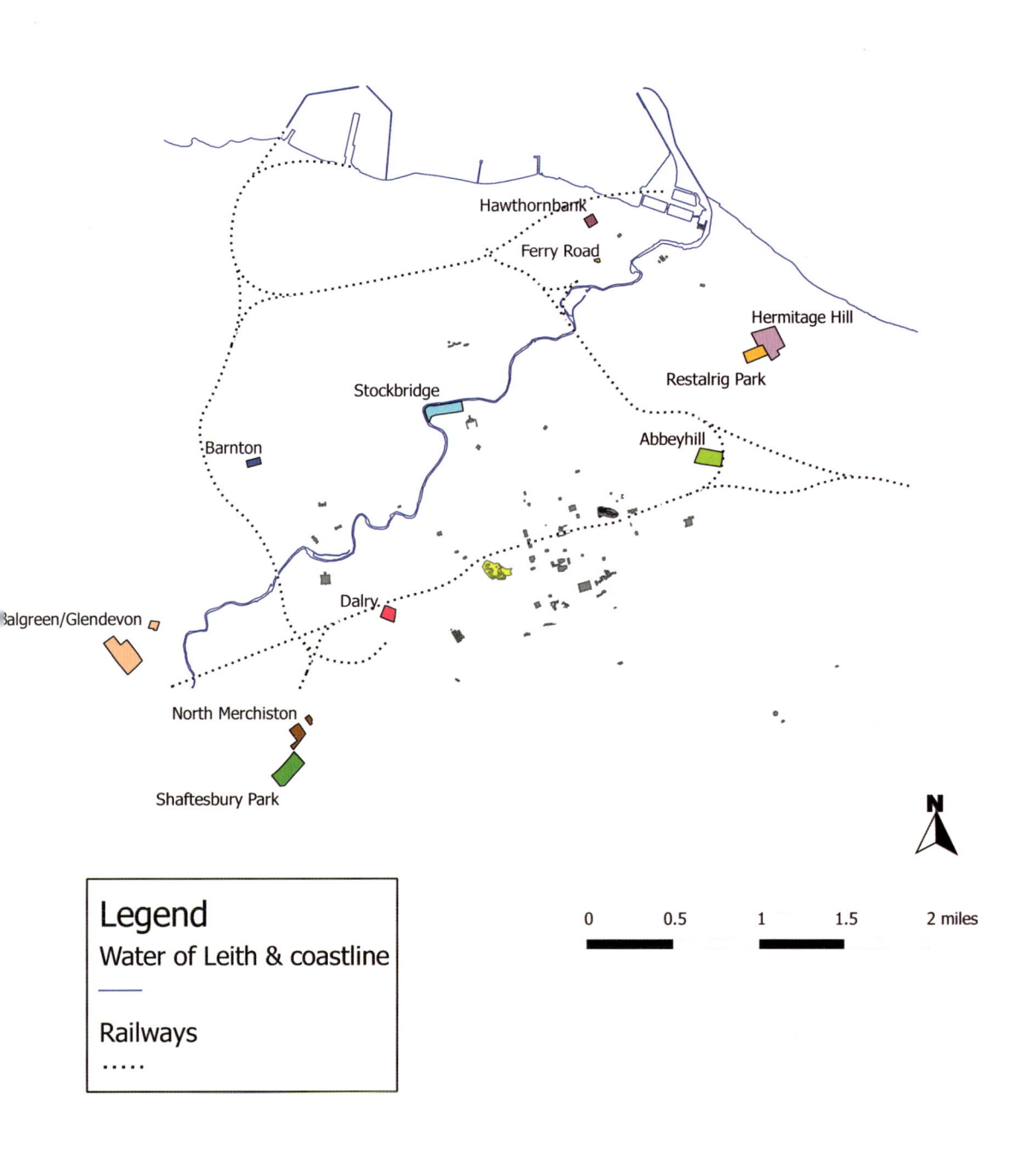

Legend
Water of Leith & coastline
―
Railways
.....

Happy Homes

Rev Dr James Begg (1808-83)
Source: Courtesy of the Scottish Reformation Society

Reid Terrace, Stockbridge
Named after an ardent Cooperative supporter, journalist, Hugh Gilzean Reid (1836-1911)

Source: J. Begg, *Happy Homes for Working Men and How to Get Them* Edinburgh 1866, frontispiece and p.32

Happy Homes*

AT 4 O'CLOCK on Wednesday 23 October 1861 the foundation stone for the first in a series of buildings to be erected by the Edinburgh Cooperative Building Company was laid by the Rev Dr James Begg. A bottle containing copies of the Edinburgh newspapers, Company regulations, and a list of shareholders was buried along with a statement about the origins of the Cooperative and a few coins. The foundation stone was then laid and the Rev Dr Begg then offered a prayer and blessed the enterprise. Construction at Reid Terrace in Stockbridge was underway.[1]

In his 2,000-word speech that followed, Begg remarked that the foundation stone was the third such ceremony in Edinburgh that day. Earlier, H.R.H. Prince Albert had officiated at the ceremonies for the Industrial Museum (now the Royal Scottish Museum, Chambers Street) and the General Post Office (Waterloo Place). 'I am quite sure,' Begg commented, 'that though this is the last in being laid, yet, so far from being the least, it is, in reality, by far the most important.' It was a 'turning point in the history of Edinburgh' and, he continued, 'We ought not to judge the stability of a nation merely by its gorgeous buildings, but we ought to judge it by the state of the great mass of the population.'

Prince Albert survived only another fifty days; the Edinburgh Cooperative Building Company (ECBC), officially and symbolically constituted on 'Independence Day', 4 July 1861, survived another eighty years and, significantly, all but a handful of the 2,300 homes built by the ECBC still survive.

* The term 'Happy Homes' comes from the publication by Rev. Dr James Begg entitled *Happy Homes for Working Men and How to Get Them* (Edinburgh, 1866).

Happy Homes

1.1 Blackfriars Wynd, Cowgate 1856
Source: Robert Chambers and James Riddel, *Traditions of Edinburgh*, Edinburgh, 1868, p.208.

1. Housing Quality and Environmental Inequality

PERHAPS Begg's view that 1861 was 'a turning point' owed something to his Free Kirk pulpit rhetoric. The reality was more gradual. For at least a quarter of a century the reading public had been introduced to some of the harsh facts of life in the Old Town. The minister of the Old Church parish, Dr Lee, testified to the *Royal Commission on Religious Instruction* in 1836 that 'he had never seen such misery. . . where the people were without furniture, without everything.' In a single day he had visited 'seven houses in which there was not a bed, in some of them not even a heap of straw.' Edwin Chadwick in his widely read *Report on the Sanitary Condition of the Labouring Population* (1842) observed that conditions of overcrowding and malnutrition lessened resistance to disease amongst the poor so that they experienced more days of sickness and gained much less weight than criminals in Edinburgh prison. Dr Tait's analysis of diseases amongst 335 individuals in Gillon's and Gibb's Closes (Canongate), Blackfriars Wynd and Skinner's Close (High Street), and Mealmarket (Cowgate) led him to conclude 'that if such an amount of sickness were known to prevail in a prison containing between 300 and 400 prisoners, the circumstance would excite public alarm and attention.'[2]

The conditions which underpinned the social and environmental inequalities in Edinburgh were well known and widely understood. The publisher William Chambers printed his thoughts on the 'many most degraded, dingy and ill-ventilated closes' in a work entitled *On the Sanitary State of the Residences of the Poorer Classes* (1840). Medical accounts of living conditions included Professor William Alison's *Observations on the Management of the Poor in Scotland* (1840) and Dr George Bell's *Day and Night in the Wynds of Edinburgh* (1849). Both captured the stark, indeed life-threatening, conditions in the Old Town. Dr Begg noted that 'about 50,000 of the people of this city are living in houses of one room, 121 of which have no windows' and '1500 houses have from six to fifteen human beings residing in them. What, asked Begg, must be the 'social state of many of the people. . . under such circumstances? How is it possible for the decencies of human life to be observed?'[3]

Public and professional awareness of living conditions was also heightened since medical students at Edinburgh University were obliged as part of their degree programme to take classes in medical jurisprudence – the study and application of scientific and medical knowledge to legal and administrative processes – and to work in a voluntary capacity in the New or Old Town Dispensaries. It was there that they practised on patients and became familiar with the conditions in which the poor survived – and died. Nationally, and internationally, many doctors active in the early public health movement were graduates of Edinburgh University and shared values and approaches developed during their student days in the city.

Edwin Chadwick commented adversely in his widely read *Report* on drainage and scavenging in Edinburgh, but reserved specific condemnation for the common stairs in high rise tenements, 'some of them exceeding ten stories' (sic):

'Another defect is. . . with common stairs, sometimes as filthy as the streets or wynds to which they open. By this construction the chance of cleanliness is lessened, the labour of carrying up necessaries, and particularly of water for the purpose of purifying is increased; and if any malaria or contagion exist in the house, the probability of its passing from dwelling to dwelling on the same stair is much greater.'[4]

William Chambers agreed: 'the construction of the town is radically unfavourable to health'. He continued:

'After a pretty exhaustive observation of the condition of towns both on the continent and in Great Britain, I am of the opinion that this city (Edinburgh) is at present one of the most uncleanly and badly ventilated in this or any adjacent country.'[5]

Tenements, the basic form of accommodation for urban Scots, were not conducive to good health. Henry Littlejohn, Police Surgeon (1854-62) and Medical Officer of Health for Edinburgh (1862-1908) produced a damning indictment of the relationship between tenement design and the public's health because 'to

1.2
William Chambers (1800-83)
Source: Reproduced with permission of Scottish Borders Council Museum and Gallery Service

1.3 High Rise High Street, Edinburgh 1827
Source: Samuel Dukinfield Swarbreck, Wiki Commons Licence

introduce waste pipes and a water supply to decaying and increasingly overcrowded multi-storey tenements was both complicated and costly'.[6] Water closets worked well in England, according to Littlejohn, 'where the poorest houses are self-contained, and necessarily small, with a court behind, in which the convenience is placed, the system works admirably'. By contrast, in centuries-old tenements the introduction of water-closets created major problems regarding leakage and blockage of sewage into the flats and stairs, and Littlejohn was strongly opposed to such a development, in contrast to the senior physician at Edinburgh Royal Infirmary, Dr William T. Gairdner, who described the provision of water as 'one of the first necessities of life'.[7]

Long before Robert Koch's bacteriological explanation, contemporaries attributed the cause of disease to 'miasma' – noxious air as identified by unpleasant smells. Indeed, waste water provoked an 'intense controversy' in 1838, known as the 'foul burn agitation' precisely because unpleasant smelling effluents and street run-off were disposed of into small open streams (burns) which, it was believed, caused epidemics.[8] As Chambers observed: 'the excrementitious matter of some forty or fifty thousand individuals is daily thrown into the gutters, at certain hours appointed by the Police Commissioners, or poured into carts which are sent about the principal streets'. Another regulation gave the Commissioners a public monopoly over 'police manure' – the collection and sale of solid waste (nightsoil) and street sweepings worth as much as £7,000 annually (£635,000 in 2022 values). Approximately 150,000 tons of solid waste was collected each year by a small army of a hundred or so scavengers and taken by canal barge westwards to Ratho or eastwards by cart through the city streets to the 'irrigated meadows' of farms at Restalrig and Craigentinny. There it was used as a fertiliser for crops which were subsequently sold and consumed in the city. With local cleansing operations funded in this way there was little incentive either for the Police Commissioners, or their successors, the Town Council, to change this arrangement.

Living conditions challenged the health of all family members. At work, some occupations were more dangerous than others – brewers, chimney sweeps, coopers, coppersmiths, porters, sawyers, and washerwomen – each experienced mortality rates double the city average. Bakers and butchers presented specific problems for consumers in the form of stale bread and diseased meat sold on their premises. Cattle plague (rinderpest) rendered beef unsuitable for human consumption, and to avoid market regulations cattlemen drove their herds beyond the city boundaries to be slaughtered and then brought the infected carcasses back for sale as though in good condition.

As for air quality, Edinburgh's nickname, 'Auld Reekie' (Old Smokey) was assigned not without reason and many smoke abatement notices were issued to breweries and industrial premises from 1848. The Infirmary was also 'a great offender'. Another environmental health 'nuisance' was burials. Cholera epidemics in 1832 and 1848 required interments in already overcrowded churchyards. Proposals for public cemeteries in the Meadows and Hunters' Bog (Arthur's Seat) came to nothing other than the flotation on the Edinburgh stock exchange of six new private profit-making burial companies, each offering burials unaffordable to the poor.[9] In death, as in life, the public's health was challenged.

Housing Quality and Environmental Inequality

1.4 Auld Reekie: smoke polluters in Edinburgh 1854

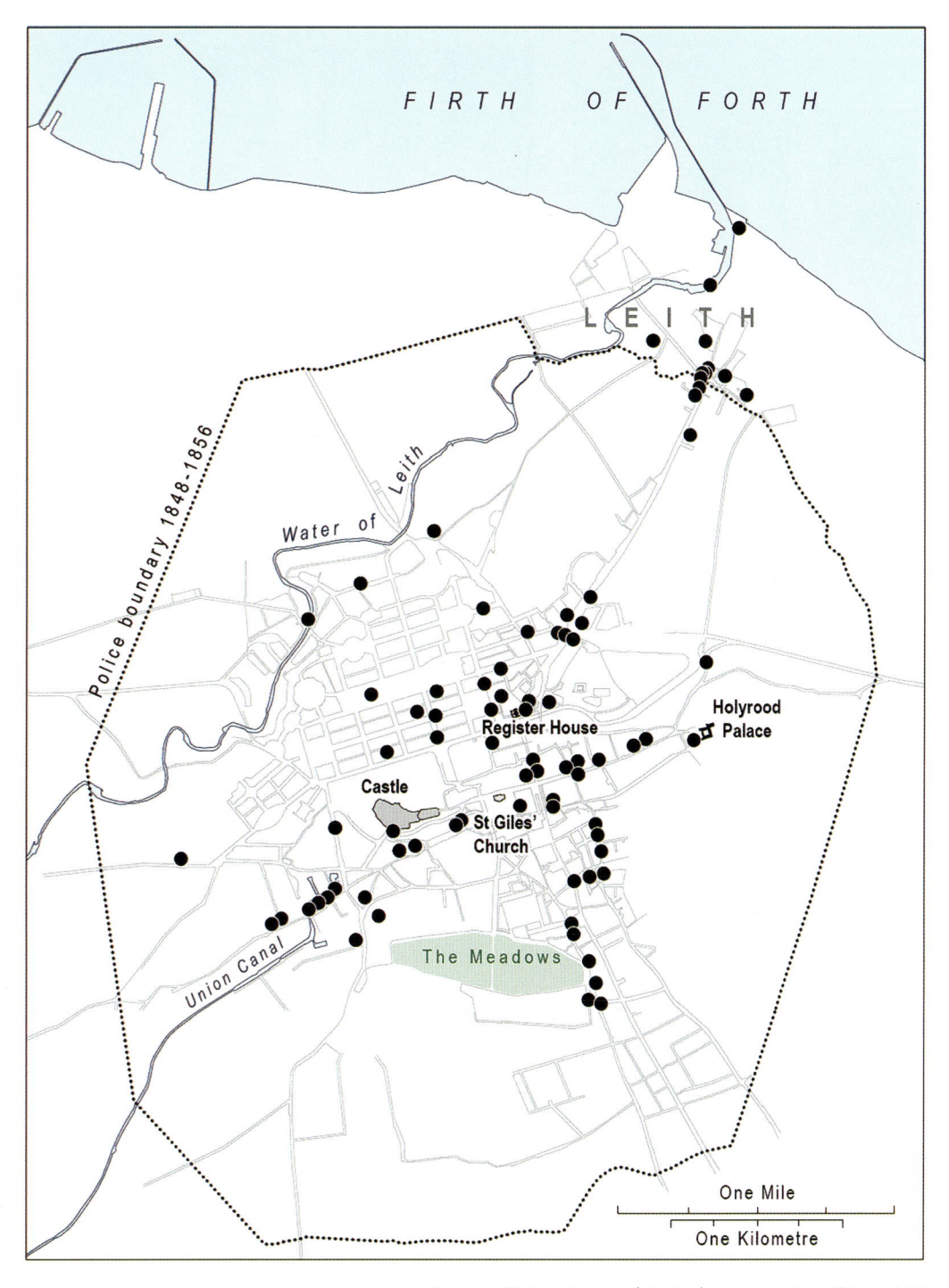

Source: © P. Laxton and R. Rodger, *Insanitary City*, p.127.

1.5 Population Growth in Edinburgh 1801-61

1801	1811	1821	1831	1841	1851	1861
67,288	82,624	112,235	136,054	138,182	160,511	168,121
	+23%	+36%	+21%	+2%	+16%	+5%

Source: Censuses of Scotland 1801-61

Most of all, deepening social inequality was particularly evident in the depreciated state of the housing stock. With sustained population growth in the first half of the nineteenth century existing living conditions in central Edinburgh came under immense pressure. Excluding Leith, the rate of increase in the 1810s, 1820s and 1830s averaged 2.5% per year (Fig.1.5). The population of Edinburgh doubled from 67,000 to 136,000 between 1801 and 1831 – equivalent nowadays to raising the current Edinburgh population to over 1 million by 2051 within the current built-up area. To put the scale of this expansion in a historical context: within the city of Edinburgh jurisdiction in 1831 the population was 51% greater than that of the city of Glasgow, and the population of the St Cuthbert's parish alone was 79% of the City of Glasgow population (Cage, 10) and larger than the burghs of Aberdeen or Dundee.[10]

The Builder captured the consequences of population growth of 25,000 in the 1840s:

> 'Divided by five, the average family size, will give us 5,007 families living in Edinburgh who were not there in 1841. To accommodate these families one of two ways must be supposed. Either 5,007 houses were unlet in 1841, or between that year and 1851, 5007 houses have been built. But what is the fact? We find in 1841, that few houses were empty; and in 1851, instead of 5,007 houses having been built, more than half that number have been knocked down. How, then, . . . have these 25,038 individuals been accommodated? The question is too easily answered: they have been closer packed.'[11]

Housing Quality and Environmental Inequality

1.6 Irish Concentrations in the Old Town 1851

Source: © P. Laxton and R. Rodger, *Insanitary City*, p.16

Main Areas of Irish Residence, Edinburgh 1851

Map ID	District	inhabitants	Irish-born	%
a	South of Victoria St	925	577	62.4
b	Cowgate	5107	1979	38.8
c	Police Chambers	2105	720	34.2
d	Grassmarket	3144	987	31.4
e	Blackfriars Wynd	4043	1264	31.3
f	West Port	88	17	19.3
g	Old St Paul's	2751	460	16.7
h	High School Yards	268	39	14.6
i	Leith Wynd	855	92	10.8
j	Candlemaker Row	514	52	10.1
k	Castlehill	653	63	9.6
l	Argyle Square	884	71	8.0
m	South Lawnmarket	396	31	7.8
n	The Bridges	676	41	6.1
o	North Lawnmarket	1830	100	5.5
p	North-west High Street	2270	108	4.8
q	High Street	980	45	4.6
r	Bank St/Market St	515	19	3.7
	All central districts	**28004**	**6665**	**23.8**

Selected Crowded Closes

Planestane's Close, 78 Grassmarket	93	84	**90.3**
Currie's Close 94, Grassmarket	282	170	**60.3**
Forrester's Wynd, 98 Cowgate	213	113	**53.1**
Pollock's Close, 28 Cowgate	64	50	**78.1**
Allison's Close, 34 Cowgate	409	288	**70.4**
Baillie's Court, 50 Cowgate	153	96	**62.7**
College Wynd, 205 Cowgate	482	226	**46.9**
Blackfriars Wynd	861	403	**46.8**
Hyndford's Close, 50 High Street	286	106	**37.1**
Toddrick's Wynd, 80 High Street	505	236	**46.7**
North Gray's Close, 125 High Street	252	97	**38.5**
Stevenlaw's Close, 134 High Street	471	188	**39.9**
Kinloch's Close, 149 High Street	52	39	**75.0**
Old Fishmarket Close, 196 High St	342	131	**38.3**

Infant mortality, a widely accepted indicator of social inequalities, was 3.6 times higher in the Old Town than in the 1850s New Town.

Two-thirds of this population increase was the result of two significant rural to urban migrations. One was the influx of Irish migrants mainly from Leitrim, Monaghan, and Cavan so that by 1851 Edinburgh housed the sixth largest concentration of Irish in mainland Britain. Numerically, Irish-born occupants of Edinburgh constituted 24% of residents in Edinburgh's courts and closes (Fig.1.6, Areas a-r) with the greatest concentrations in the Cowgate, Grassmarket, and High Street areas. In each of Planestane's, Pollock's, Alison's, and Kinloch's Closes more than 70% of residents were Irish-born; almost half the 1360 residents in Toddrick's and Blackfriars Wynds on Census night, Sunday 30 March 1851, were also Irish-born, and significant clusters also congregated in the closes of the South and North Back of the Canongate.

However, to label overcrowding and living conditions as an Irish issue is simplistic. Another influx of migrants from the eastern and southern Scottish Highlands was of agricultural workers, displaced by landowners and changing farming methods. With no right to poor relief in Scotland and no formal assessment of need, as was the case in England, there was little incentive for the rural poor to remain in the parish of their birth. 'The poor in Scotland, especially in Edinburgh and Glasgow', Friedrich Engels explained 'are worse off than any other region of the three kingdoms.' And as if to ensure that the Irish were not unfairly blamed, he added: 'the poorest are not Irish, but Scottish.'[12]

Poor relief in Scotland was minimalist in comparison to England where the costs of pauperism were met by property owners who paid poor rates. There was no such system in Scotland. Able-bodied men and childless women were ineligible for poor relief. Instead, as the Royal Commission on the Poor Law reported in 1844, parsimonious Presbyterianism prospered with the 'discriminating hand of charity' used by the kirk to address moral improvement.[13] As a later account put it:

> 'The law of Scotland. . . is that when a man has been starved to the point of illness and incapacity to work he may be relieved at the public cost, but so long as he retains so much physical strength that he can be called able-bodied he must be allowed to starve.'[14]

There was some evidence, also, to suggest that both Roman Catholic and Presbyterian clergy used soup kitchens to encourage church attendance and, on occasions, a change of religious adherence. Mr Farrel, for example, living in Castle Hill, was 'a Roman Catholic but uniformly attentive to Protestant instructions', according to Mr Frazer, a visitor employed by the Edinburgh Society for the Relief of Indigent Old Men (founded 1806).

Lacking a formal system of poor relief, charity was provided in a casual manner through a variety of Edinburgh organisations. Oliver and Boyd's *Almanac* recorded an increase from 30 to 54 non-medical charities in Edinburgh between 1837 and 1860.[15] Even the Town Council, despite its financial problems, funded poor relief for men by employing them to break stones and lay paths and roads around the Meadows and the Queen's Park. For women, children and the aged the Council also provided soup kitchens which in the winter of 1838-39 served 12,000-15,000 people daily. Civil societies such as the Society for the Relief of Indigent Old Men, and the Destitute Sick Societies, were also active. Perhaps the most comprehensive efforts were made by a relatively new organisation, the Edinburgh City Mission (ECM) founded in 1832.[16] Modelled on a Glasgow City Mission (1827) established by David Nasmith, this non-denominational organisation took a radical approach to the relief of poverty. City missionaries were not theologically trained, and the ECM challenged the assumption that Britain did not need missionaries because it was a 'Christian' country. With the extraordinary energy of six privately funded urban missionaries, the first ECM Annual Report (1834) stated that 2,178 meetings were held which 39,377 people attended; 16,873 homes were visited; 5,488 sick people visited; and 12,837 tracts distributed.

According to Professor Alison, 11.6% of the Edinburgh population were destitute; they had no lawful means of subsistence and so were forced to live on alms. He explained to the Statistical Society of London in 1842, 'where there is no effective legal provision for the poor. . . there is much unrelieved or imperfectly relieved destitution'. He continued: 'the natural effect of this is, not prudence, but degradation, and the natural effect of degradation is improvidence, recklessness, and thereby a morbid increase of population'. Consequently, 'not only the sufferings of the poor, but. . . the numbers of the suffering poor' were much greater in Scotland than in England. Dearth and death, disease and debility were linked, as Alison noted:

> 'Let us look to the closes of Edinburgh. . . and thoroughly understand the character and habits, the diseases and mortality, of the unemployed poor, unprotected by the law, who gather there from all parts of the country; let us study the condition of the aged and disabled poor. . . let us compare these things with the provisions for the poor, not only in England but in many other Christian countries; so far from priding ourselves on the smallness of the sums which are applied to this purpose in Scotland we must honestly and candidly confess, that our parsimony in this particular is equally injurious to the poor and discreditable to the rich in Scotland.'

Infant mortality rate (child deaths less than 1 year old) amongst professional families was 72/1000; for merchants families it was almost double at 127/1000; and amongst the families of labourers infant mortality was more than triple that of professionals at 241/1000 (Fig.1.7). Destitution contributed directly in Edinburgh to an annual mortality rate 10% above that of Liverpool – the highest rate recorded in England. It also had a distinctly occupational and class-based character as the statistician James Stark showed in 1847. Throughout the life course, from cradle to grave, survival rates in Edinburgh were strongly correlated with occupation. The 'death penalty' of class- and occupationally-based differentials in survival rates continued undiminished for most of the lifespan.

The preponderance in the Old Town of an unskilled, low paid, irregularly employed labouring class lacking access to poor relief was in stark contrast to the New Town parishes of St Andrew's, St George's, St Mary's and St Stephen's where the presence of what the Census officially termed 'capitalists, bankers and educated men' enjoyed steady incomes from salaries and annuities. Edinburgh was socially, residentially, and occupationally segregated by design and the Census Report in 1831 said as much (Fig.1.8).

The Edinburgh middle classes were concerned in general terms with how living conditions affected public order, morality, and religiosity – probably in that order! This was precisely why they sought to detach themselves from the perceived physical and moral contamination of the Old Town by developing a New Town with its

Housing Quality and Environmental Inequality

1.7 Survival of the Fittest?
Mortality by Type of Employment, Edinburgh 1841

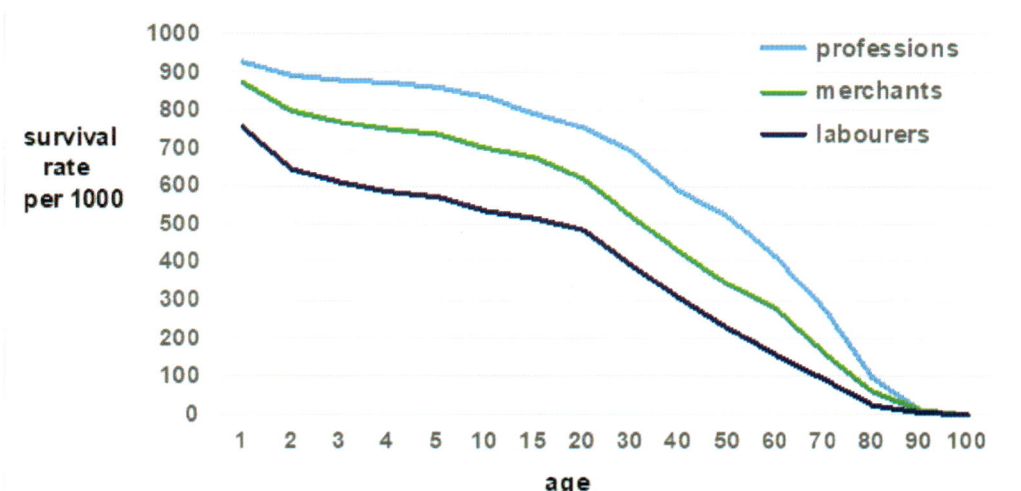

Source: J. Stark, *Inquiry into some points of the Sanatory State of Edinburgh* (Edinburgh, 1847), p.25

1.8 Occupational Segregation: 'Capitalists' and Labourers, 1831

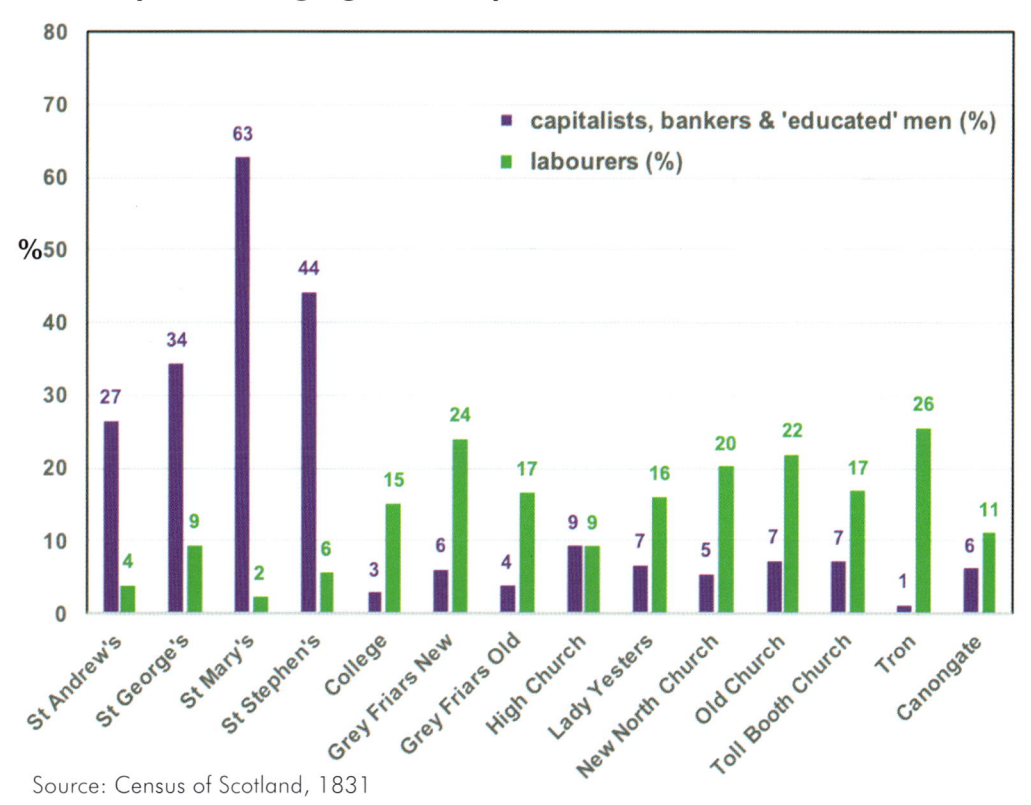

Source: Census of Scotland, 1831

assembly rooms, gentlemen's clubs, and a rival school, The Edinburgh Academy, to insulate their sons against a twice-daily trek through the contaminated Cowgate to High School Yards. More specifically, fear of cholera epidemics (1832, 1848) and contagious diseases in general prompted those with sufficient income to quit the central districts. To relocate, therefore, was a logical survival strategy since the premature death of the household head or his sons adversely affected the income, wealth, and prospects of all surviving family members.

2.1 The incomplete Stonework at Saxe Coburg Place
a continuing reminder of the financial collapse of 1825

2. Arrested Development

THE HOUSING market, already under unprecedented pressure from sustained population expansion after 1800, encountered another serious blow. A stock market crash in London in 1825, prompted by unsecured overseas lending in South America by the Bank of England, resulted in the failure of six London and sixty county banks in England. Though the impact in Scotland was less dramatic there were high profile casualties, notably Sir Walter Scott and the publishing houses of John Murray, and Constable and Ballantyne.[1] Scottish financial independence, guaranteed by the Act of Union, was perceived as threatened, though in reality the small scale of Scottish banking was under 'watchful superintendence' and fortnightly reporting.[2]

Locally, the availability and cost of borrowing increased due to the international crash. Commercial activity, and construction particularly, experienced a serious depression in the second quarter of the nineteenth century. Had Begg turned round in 1861 after he gave his oration at Reid Terrace he could have looked up to see the incomplete stonework of 15 Saxe Coburg Place, an abrupt interruption to building work there, and a reminder of the financial collapse in 1825. Had Begg lived another century and walked along architect Patrick Wilson's Hopetoun Crescent he would have still seen the only four homes built in the street at numbers 7, 8, 17 and 18, and still easily identifiable today' (Fig.2.1).[3] No further properties were built before the end of the century! W. H. Playfair's ambitious plan (1819) for the north side of London Road was limited in the 1830s to Leopold Place, Elm Row and a few partially completed terraced houses in Hillside Crescent. Stark, ragged stonework and gap sites around the city memorialised the vulnerability of the building trades as exposed by the financial crash. Nowhere was such pressure more apparent

2.2 Hope Crescent Incomplete 1949

© Reproduced with the permission of the National Library of Scotland (NLS) OS large scale 1/1250 town plan 1949

than at Saxe Coburg Place when in 1828 the developer James Milne was forced to sell, and his successor Adam Turnbull also came under financial pressure and declared bankrupt in 1834.

Elsewhere in Edinburgh, the financial crisis brought an abrupt and prolonged halt to new housing developments. At Tollcross, building work ceased on the Brougham and Home Streets sites of James Home Rigg's Drumdryan estate, and tenement building nearby on Tarvit and Drumdryan streets had to wait another forty years for completion. Developments begun in 1822 on Bread Street and across Lothian Road at St Anthony's Place (now the east end of Morrison Street) ceased, and William Burn's 1825 feuing plan for the Castle Terrace area of the Grindlay Orchardfield estate made no real progress until the 1860s.[4]

Similarly, the proposal to complete a mirror image of Gardner's Crescent (1822) was aborted, and the plans for an elegant development nearby at Grove Square literally never got off the ground. Nor, as might have been expected with the completion of new trans-

2.3 Arrested Development: Annual Increase in Feu Duties (£) on Heriot's Trust Lands 1800–60*

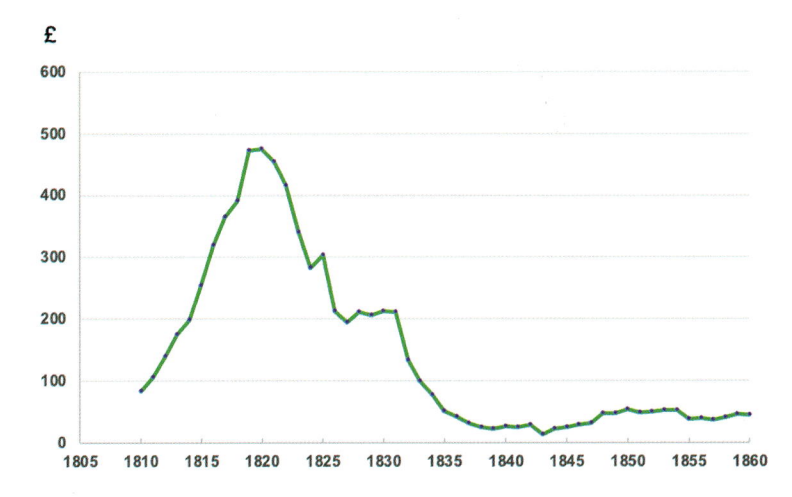

*Note: 7-year moving average
Source: Richard Rodger, The Transformation of Edinburgh, p.77.

port hubs at the Union Canal basin (1822) and Haymarket Station (1842), nor did a stimulus to housebuilding result. Indeed, Manor Place remained the western 'frontier' of the city into the early 1850s with country houses at East and West Cotes and orchards at Dalry.

A powerful indicator of the impact of the financial crisis on new housebuilding in Edinburgh can be seen through the experience of Heriot's Trustees, the largest landowner and property developer in the city. Heriot's receipts ('feu' duties) on the release of mainly New Town land for development experienced an abrupt and sustained decline from a peak in the early 1820s (Fig.2.3).

With the pace of population growth expanding in the second quarter of the nineteenth century at a rate never before – or later – achieved; with severely limited additions to housing supply, an extended economic recession, an inconsistent approach to poor relief, endemic fever, and cholera epidemics in 1832 and 1847-48, then to say that living conditions in the older areas of Edinburgh deteriorated significantly in the second quarter of the nineteenth century is a gross understatement. The balance of supply and demand tipped firmly in favour of property owners rather than tenants, and the Old Town was 'hollowed out' by the flight of its wealthier professional and merchant classes.

Happy Homes

3.1 The Disruption of the Church of Scotland and the Signing of the Deed of Demission, 1843
by David Octavius Hill, WiKi Commons Licence

3. Verbal Battlegrounds

MOUNTING empirical evidence published by *The Scotsman* in the 1830s and 1840s linked fever to overcrowded housing and poverty.[1] The underlying logic of these and other press reports by the *Scottish Guardian, North British Review, Chambers' Edinburgh Journal* and *Edinburgh Magazine*, as well as from the Royal Colleges of Physicians and Surgeons, was that unemployment diminished the likelihood of the family to be properly nourished. As poverty gripped the household budget, the family increased its reliance on stale bread, watered milk, and diseased meat 'greedily bought up' at 4d rather than 9d per pound from carts on a Saturday night.[2] Their resistance to infection and disease was further diminished, as was their capacity for work. The poverty spiral intensified.[3] Bouts of unemployment became longer. Rents, as the largest component of the family budget, offered most scope to economise yet the overcrowding that resulted from scaling back domestic space and amenities only increased exposure to infection. That limited further a worker's ability to obtain and retain work. It was the poverty *cycle* that was endemic.

Within this frame of reference poverty was at the centre of public health and community well-being, argued Professor Alison. An improved domestic environment was considered critical to address the morbidity of the urban population. Keeping people in work, or at least temporarily providing them with charitable contributions either from voluntary sources or poor law relief, was Alison's preferred strategy to address health and insanitary housing.[4] It was an under-consumptionist explanation of unemployment of which John Maynard Keynes would have approved a century later. *The Scotsman* referred to 'the unquestionable force' of Alison's argument, and the periodical press were all in agreement. It was an approach that was consistent with Henry Duncan Littlejohn's tenure as Edinburgh's first Police Surgeon (1854-62).[5]

Interrupted incomes, infrequent incomes, or inadequate incomes, however described, each contributed to the plight of the urban

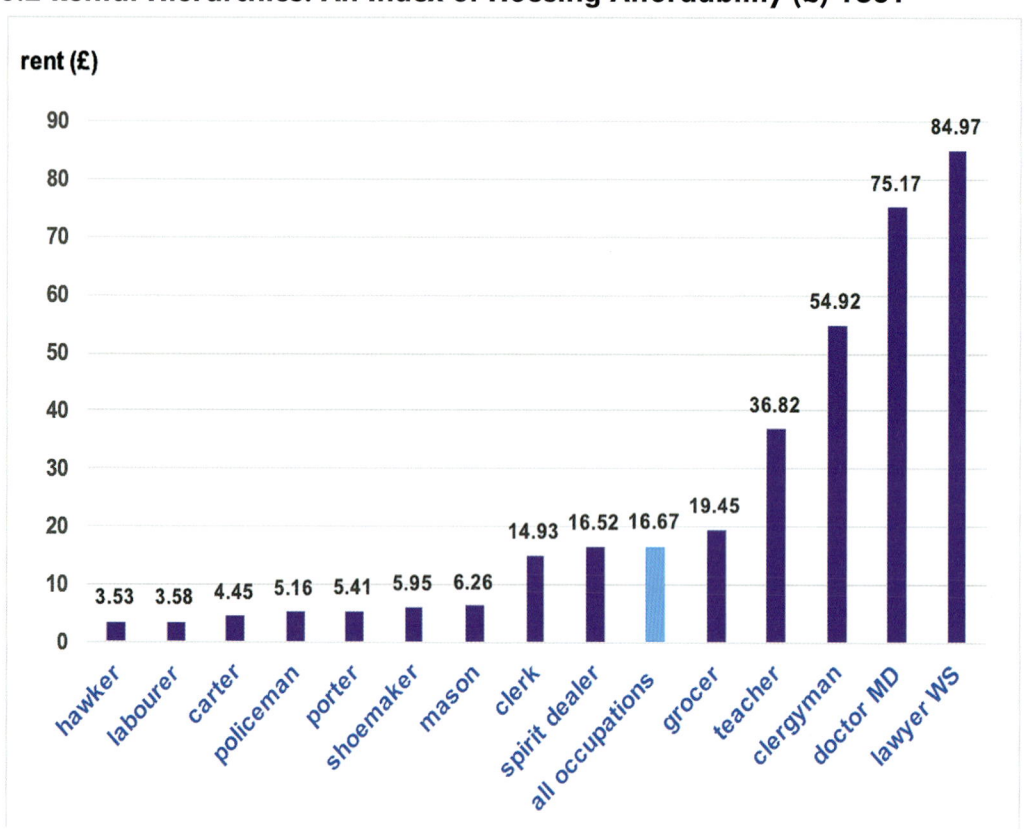

3.2 Rental Hierarchies: An Index of Housing Affordability (£) 1861*

Occupation	Rent (£)
hawker	3.53
labourer	3.58
carter	4.45
policeman	5.16
porter	5.41
shoemaker	5.95
mason	6.26
clerk	14.93
spirit dealer	16.52
all occupations	16.67
grocer	19.45
teacher	36.82
clergyman	54.92
doctor MD	75.17
lawyer WS	84.97

Source: National Records of Scotland (NRS), Valuation Rolls, Edinburgh 1860-61, VR100/33-37

*Selected from a list of 900 occupations as described by male household heads of Edinburgh properties

poor. This can be seen in summary form through the rents affordable by tenants in a variety of occupations. Quarrying the Valuation Rolls for 1861 provides a snapshot of over 23,000 rental properties in Edinburgh at precisely the moment when the Edinburgh Cooperative Building Company was formed. This reveals an average annual rent payable of £16.67 but obscures the reality that 83% of homes were rented below that, and that half the households in Edinburgh paid no more than £5.50 per annum – the median rent. In practice, rents were indications of the affordability of workers' homes for the forthcoming year and when considered in connection with individual streets provides a rental contour map of the city and the clustering of the disadvantaged (Fig.3.2). When considering the activities of the Edinburgh Cooperative Building Company it is important to bear in mind these average rental levels in the city and what was affordable by working class families.

In contrast to Alison, what would nowadays be called a 'behaviouralist' view, the Rev Dr Thomas Chalmers and a group of evangelical ministers, which included the Rev Dr James Begg, claimed that housing conditions were the product of character defects. Immigrants, Irish and highlanders, were amongst those scapegoated for their rough, often rural, behaviour and personal habits which created insanitary housing and were fundamentally linked to poverty. The solution to the urban crisis, they claimed, was for the Church of Scotland to reassert its waning spiritual and moral supervision over the crowded populations of nineteenth century Scottish towns and cities.[6] To achieve this the pastoral mission was reinvigorated, and it was the responsibility of the Church exclusively to appoint ministers to achieve it. The approach, promoted by Chalmers as convener of the Church of Scotland's Committee on Church Extension from 1834, was based on the traditional characteristics of the rural parochial ministry: regular household visits by elders who took responsibility for the governance and discipline of the church locally; a system of day and Sunday schools; a ministry focused on small, clearly-defined parishes and congregations; and parish-based poor relief financed exclusively by church door collections and voluntary contributions. The principle of atomised churches, 'the godly commonwealth', each with a congregation of about 2,000 souls was considered from 1838 as the spatial basis on which to revive the social structure of closely-knit Christian communities.[7]

3.3 Rev Dr Thomas Chalmers (1780-1847)

3.4 Professor William P. Alison (1790-1859)
Source: Courtesy of Royal College of Physicians of Edinburgh

Professor Alison and Rev Dr Thomas Chalmers fought an oratorical duel in a debate at a meeting of the British Association for the Advancement of Science in Glasgow in 1840. In a highly charged public environment, with extensive newspaper coverage, Alison insisted that poverty was not a character defect but a casualty of a new urban economic and industrial order in which 23,000 persons or 1 in 6 of the population of Edinburgh were so impoverished in 1841 that they were dependent on alms for some part of the year.[8] Chalmers recommended a crusade to revive religious responsibility, and his eloquence eclipsed the empirical evidence from medical reports produced by Alison. Despite their intense opposition, personal relations between protagonists were cordial since 'they recognised the other as having reached an opposite conclusion within a common framework.'[9]

The evangelists' emphasis was on supportive communities, educational instruction, moral improvement, and self-help. They were fundamentally opposed to the Poor Law ('a moral gangrene') and workhouses ('pauper bastilles') to address poverty. After 'Ten Years Conflict' Chalmers and the evangelical ministers seceded from the Church of Scotland on 18th May 1843 in protest at what they viewed as interference by the state in the religious responsibility of the Church to appoint ministers and define their duties. Irreconcilable differences within the Church of Scotland led to a schism. The result was a walk-out of 474 ministers (37%) and General Assembly delegates who then morphed into the Free Church of Scotland, under their first Moderator Rev Dr Thomas Chalmers, and held a parallel General Assembly at Tanfield (Canonmills).[10]

The Disruption has been described as 'by far the most spectacular split. . . in British church history.'[11] Between 1835 and 1851, the Church of Scotland's share of Sunday service attendances fell catastrophically from 44% to 16%; by contrast, Free Church attendance rocketed to 37%, and United Presbyterians accounted for 25%. The established Church of Scotland had become a minority sect by 1851, outnumbered four to one by the other Presbyterian churches. It was a crisis of faith in the city if not an existential threat to the Church of Scotland. In the long run, this intra-Presbyterian strife was also a political conduit for liberal views to gain traction and led to the formation of a Liberal Party in Edinburgh and across Scotland that held political sway until the First World War.[12]

Verbal Battlegrounds

New College, Mound Place built 1845-50 as a church and theological college for the Free Church by W. H. Playfair
WiKi Commons Licence

Happy Homes

Fig 4.1 Boundary Complexities in Edinburgh before 1856

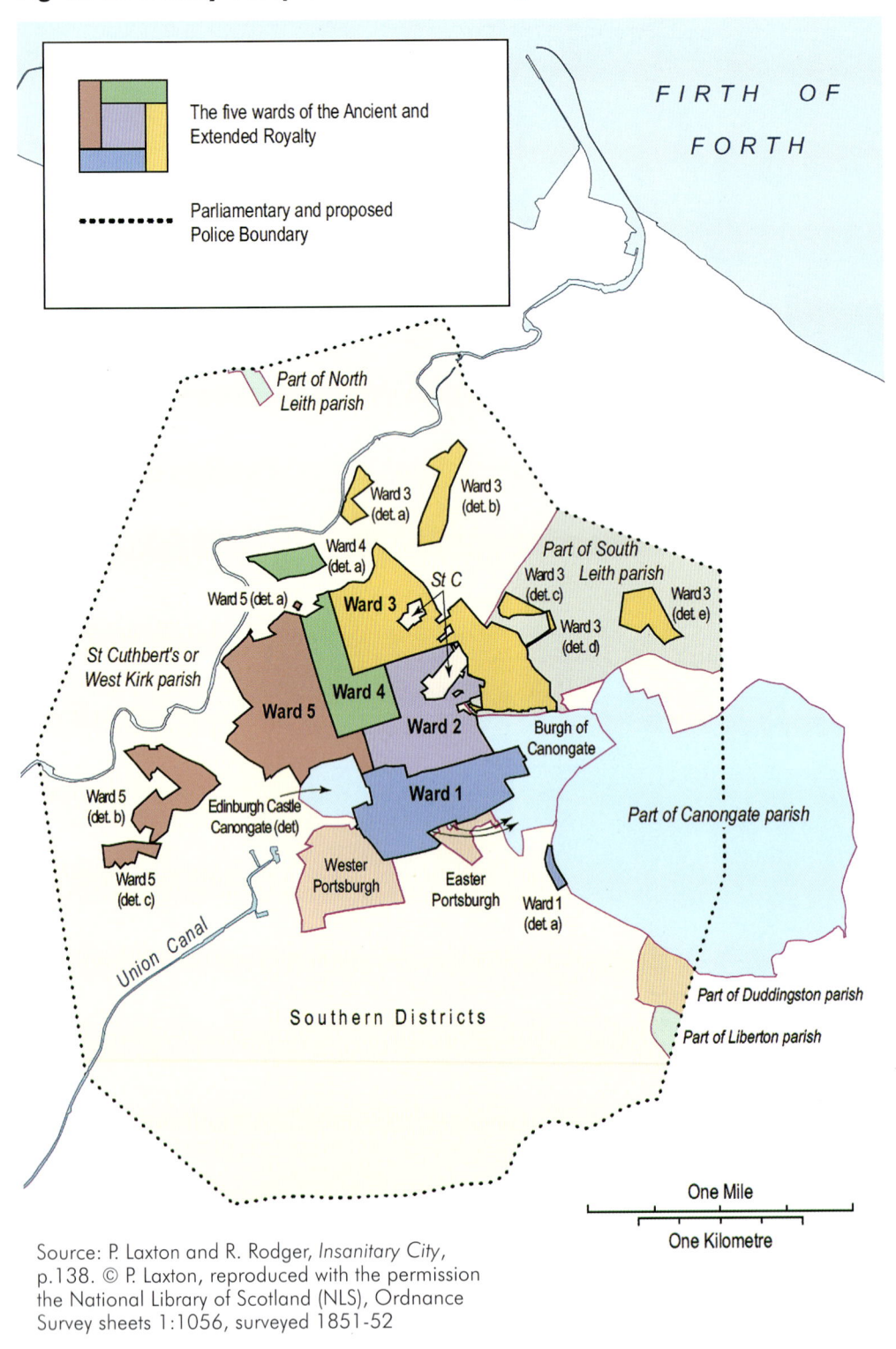

Source: P. Laxton and R. Rodger, *Insanitary City*, p.138. © P. Laxton, reproduced with the permission the National Library of Scotland (NLS), Ordnance Survey sheets 1:1056, surveyed 1851-52

4. Re-thinking the City

THE SECOND quarter of the nineteenth century began with a serious financial crisis and economic retrenchment in Edinburgh. Population pressure was intense, but the rate of growth slackened appreciably in the 1830s with just 2% more inhabitants than at the start of the decade – the lowest decennial increase in the entire nineteenth century. The population rebound in the 1840s was modest (+15%) and in-migration was mainly of distressed Irish and displaced rural Scots. Twin cholera epidemics in 1832 and 1848 showed little respect for class and status, though the physically weakened and financial straitened were more susceptible in the congested courts and towering tenements.

Public administration in the city was chaotic. Responsibility for epidemic disease was split amongst the Police Surgeon (medical issues); the Inspector of Cleaning (scavenging and lime-washing of passages); and the Parochial Boards (internal fumigation and cleaning). The arrangement demonstrated the futility of public health administration where 'several authorities co-existed in barely disguised hostility'.[1] Also responsibility for budgetary management in the City Chamberlain's department had been so chaotic that a financial package from the Treasury in London had been necessary in 1838 to rescue the insolvent City Council. Even after this debacle it remained unclear 'in what proportions the [city of Edinburgh's] bankruptcy was a consequence of fraud, of incompetent book-keeping, of poor financial administration and arrangement, of over-optimism, and of extravagance'.[2]

The third quarter of the nineteenth century began with four major institutional changes in four consecutive years. If the Free Church of Scotland sought to manage the moral well-being of the population the civic state was increasingly empowered to develop the amenities and resources to do so in many spheres of daily life. Firstly, in 1853 a detailed Ordnance Survey of Edinburgh provided a map of the city which rendered it more 'legible' in the sense of understanding its spatial characteristics and relationships.[3] Secondly, in 1854, a systematic re-organisation of local taxation was introduced with yearly updates to the Valuation Roll.[4] Thirdly, in 1855, legislation replacing parish registers by compulsory civil registration as the official record of births, deaths and marriages brought Edinburgh and Scotland into line with England.[5] And finally, in 1856, the Edinburgh Municipality Extension Act confirmed the city as what would now be called a 'unitary authority.'[6] Semi-detached, semi-autonomous areas – Portsburgh, Calton and the extensive, tax-rich Southern Districts and St Cuthbert's – were incorporated within the official Edinburgh boundaries and thus became part of the city's formal jurisdictional responsibility.

The city became a more coherent and legitimate single administrative body. The Town Council which in 1856 replaced the dual responsibilities of the Corporation and Police Commission brought with it the potential for more decisive urban management.[7] Church *administration* and civil *administration* based on the parish as an administrative unit were no longer synonymous; they were essentially decoupled as these different authorities each began to 're-think' their approach to the city.

Independently of administrative reorganisation, Free Church ministers in Edinburgh embarked on a post-Disruption programme of public engagement centred on housing issues. A flurry of religious tracts and social commentaries signalled the Free Church's new mission.[8] No one was more active or influential than Rev Dr James Begg. In *Pauperism and the Poor Laws* (1849), ominously subtitled 'Our sinking population and rapidly increasing public burdens practically considered', Begg reaffirmed the Free Church's practical opposition to the Poor Law and stressed the creed of personal responsibility to minister to the disadvantaged in society. Embedded in *Pauperism and the Poor Laws* was an eight-point charter which sought to provide better quality dwellings with improved amenities such as washing houses and bleaching greens and to make them affordable to the lower paid through a reduction in the price of land and conveyancing costs.

4.2 Rev Dr William Garden Blaikie (1820-99)

Theologian, writer, Temperance reformer, Moderator of the General Assembly of the Free Church of Scotland (1892)

Source: https://commons.wikimedia.org/w/index.php?curid=4832480, CC BY-SA 3.0

4.3 Pilrig Cottages 1851

Note: Leith Walk is at the bottom right-hand corner
Source: Reproduced with the permission of NLS OS large scale town plan, 1849-53

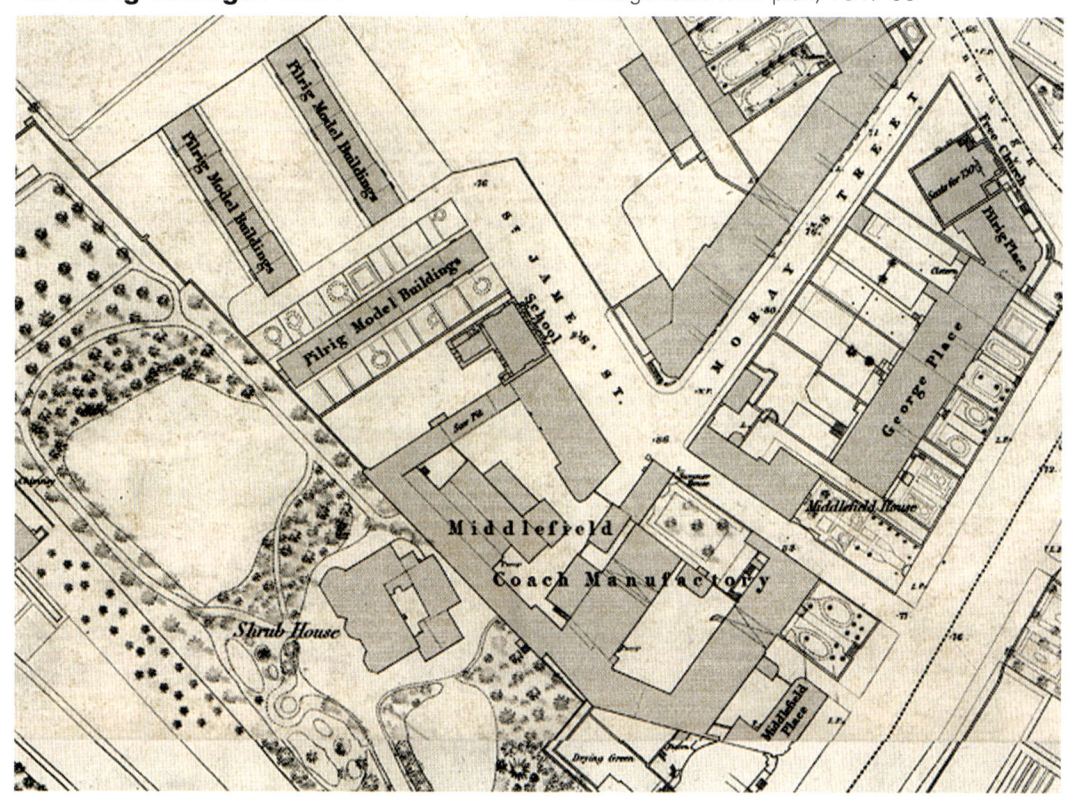

4.4 Pilrig Cottages, Shaw's Place

Begg's eight points were:

1. Improvement in the quantity and quality of education
2. Suppression of drunkenness
3. Better dwellings for working people
4. Public washing houses and bleaching greens
5. Reform of land laws
6. Simplification of the transference of land
7. Different treatment for crime and pauperism
8. Greater justice to Scotland in Parliament

Begg's 1849 charter influenced the Committee set up by the Free Church of Scotland in 1858 to investigate housing conditions and moral reform.[9] But in the short term, Charter points 2, 3, 4 and 7 were promoted by principled individuals and organisations. Amongst the first to act was the Pilrig Model Buildings Association, founded in 1849, with guidance from their Free Church minister Rev Dr William Blaikie, another of the 474 secessionists in the

Disruption of 1843. Designed by the architect Patrick Wilson,[10] the Association built 28 stone cottages in 1850 and 1851 near Pilrig Street. The result, Shaw Street, was composed of a pair of parallel two-storey blocks. Flats on the ground floor were accessed from one side of the building while those on the upper floor by the stairs on the other side of the block. The flats were self-contained, normally with two rooms, a scullery, gas and water supplies, a W.C. shared with another family, and a small garden plot outside each entrance. Another line of 16 cottages (Shaw Place) was built in 1850, and eventually to complete the court development around the gardens, another 18 cottages were constructed in 1862 (Shaw Terrace). With a marble works nearby, it was perhaps unsurprising that 'marble cutter' was the second most common occupation after 'clerk' amongst men living in Pilrig Buildings in 1861. Skilled work was also available in Middlefield Coach Manufactory, and in printing and paper-making premises all within a short walk from Pilrig Buildings.

Only two of the Pilrig household heads were general labourers. With their lower and more volatile incomes, and greater susceptibility to economic recessions, rents in Pilrig Model Dwellings houses were generally unaffordable to this occupational category. So steady employment was already perceived by workers as a critical first step to housing improvement. Professor Alison, one of the Pilrig managers, must have felt vindicated.[11]

Working at least 54 hours per week occupied the principal breadwinner fully; it kept him away from the public house, and a close-knit neighbourhood-based community used moral force to hold occupants to account for their behaviour. Sermons resonating from pulpits reinforced the importance of sobriety and piety. In print there was no let up to the urban mission. Like Begg, the Rev Dr William Blaikie was a prolific pamphleteer. His *Six Lectures Addressed to the Working Classes on the Improvement of their Temporal Condition* (1849), subsequently published as *Better Days for Working People* (1863), sold over 60,000 copies (!) and was designed as an instructional guide for an artisanal class in mid-century Pilrig and elsewhere.

On All Saints Day, 1 November 1850, Pilrig Model Dwellings, then in the process of construction, were visited by Lord Ashley,

4.5 Ashley Buildings

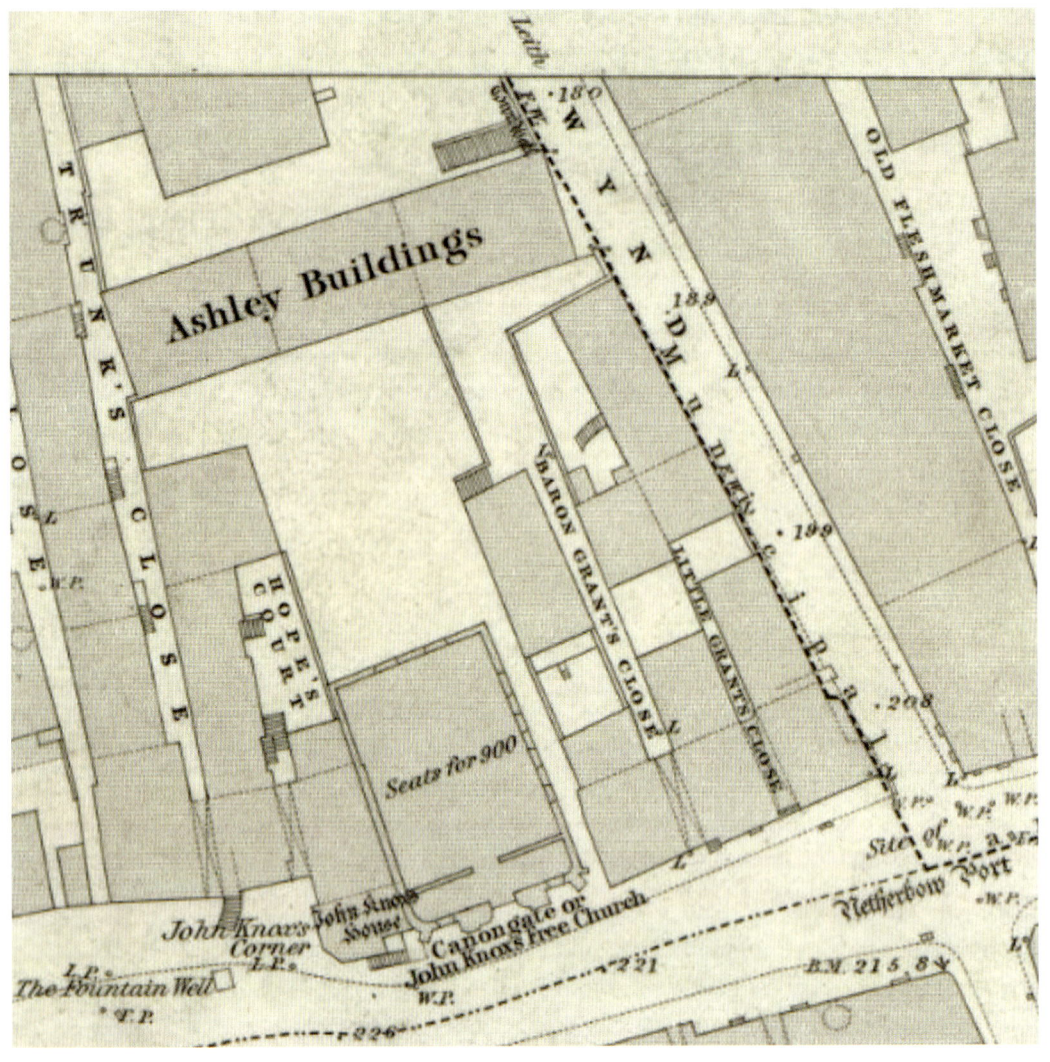

Source: Reproduced with the permission of NLS OS large scale town plan, 1849-53

a social reformer with a national profile.[12] After 'minutely examining the houses' together with the architect and committee, Ashley was 'particularly struck by the ingenuity and completeness of the plan by which each residence has a separate outside door with a plot of garden ground attached'.[13] His views were also sought regarding the plans for a large new building intended to accommodate forty families to a standard equivalent to the Metropolitan Association in London. The cost was approximately £5000, of which 80% was already subscribed, and the building was located behind John Knox's High Street house, and subsequently known as Ashley Buildings.

Without doubt the visit to Edinburgh in 1850 by a prominent national figure provided a confidence boost to housing improvers locally. Another public event reinforced that impact. The Rev Dr Thomas Guthrie, 'a zealous Free Churchman'[14] and founder of the non-sectarian Edinburgh Ragged Schools, Castle Hill (1847) invited Lord Ashley in his capacity as President of the London Ragged School Union to address a public meeting on 'the lost and outcast' in the city.[15] The potentially adverse effects of family circumstances on child development were widely known in Edinburgh and Lord Ashley remarked on the tendency of epidemics to affect those aged between 24 and 32 and how that in turn impacted adversely on children who were then either orphaned or left in a wretched condition.[16] This, he explained, underpinned the philosophy of Ragged Schools:

> 'It is not that we intend to keep those ragged who come into these schools. Our object is to receive them ragged and turn them out clothed, as it is our object to receive them as heathens and send them out as Christians.'
>
> Source: *The Scotsman*, 2 Nov. 1850, p.4.

4.6 Anthony Ashley Cooper, 7th Earl of Shaftesbury (1801-85)
Source: Wikipedia, Wellcome V0005401, CC By 4.0 Stipple engraving by J. Brown, https://wellcomeimages.org/indexplus/image

Refurbishment of mind and body were seen as inter-linked in what nowadays would be considered cases of multiple deprivation.

Some individuals engaged directly and personally with the problem of housing poverty. For example, Dr Robert Foulis, an informed, well-heeled surgeon resident at 144 Princes Street[17] refurbished Hatter's Land (now Warden's Close) at the junction of Grassmarket and Cowgatehead. By building houses with a water supply, bleaching green, grocer's premises, coffee house, reading room, and a lodging house for artisans, and by banning drink, Foulis transformed this former cholera black spot.[18] 'To this hour', Dr Littlejohn wrote in 1862, 'the close in question stands out an oasis amidst the wretchedness and filth that is to be met with in the other closes of that well-known locality.'[19]

4.7 Rev Dr Thomas Guthrie DD, FRSE (1808-83)

Sometimes it was only possible to provide temporary relief. Those who were homeless might seek communal night shelters such as provided by the Victoria Lodging Houses (Table 4.1). This was intended to assist families, migrants, and an underclass of casually and irregularly employed workers. The Night Asylum for

Table 4.1 Victoria Lodging Houses 1850

	Number of Lodgers 15 December 1850			
	Men	Women	Children	Total
West Port House	350	14	73	71
Merchant Street House	38	194	54	286
Cowgate House	536	-	-	536
total	924	208	61	1193

Source: *The Scotsman*, 21 December, 1850, p.2.

the Houseless averaged 40 persons every night throughout the year, 31% of whom could neither read nor write, and like breakfast missions, parish hand-outs, medical and charitable organisations generally, these institutions offered only temporary respite.[20] They did not address systemic weaknesses.

Sometimes, public assistance was essential. This was often the case in winter when employment was severely curtailed by daylight hours and weather. For example, the unemployment situation between February and late-April 1858 was extreme, and private donations totalling about £1,100 were managed by public authorities to provide over 12,500 workdays for men at 6d (2.5p) per day for breaking stones and laying roads at the Meadows, Castle bank, the Radical Road (Arthur's Seat), Calton Hill, and other sites in the city.[21]

None of the housing initiatives in the early 1850s addressed the scale and extent of the housing problem in Edinburgh. A correspondent for *The Builder*, a highly regarded and widely read national journal, commented that 'the most necessitous of the working classes are not benefited by such efforts' and, in a particularly damning comment, remarked that he had not seen 'such a degree and extent of wretchedness. . . during his long residence on the Continent'.[22] Even though 'demand for the (Pilrig) houses has been at least six times equal to supply' the financial and structural 'models' were unlikely to be successful despite the best intentions of the distinguished management committee.[23]

Further housing initiatives developed in the early 1850s. One, Chalmers Buildings in Fountainbridge, begun in 1854, shared many of the characteristics of the Pilrig scheme. Patrick Wilson was again

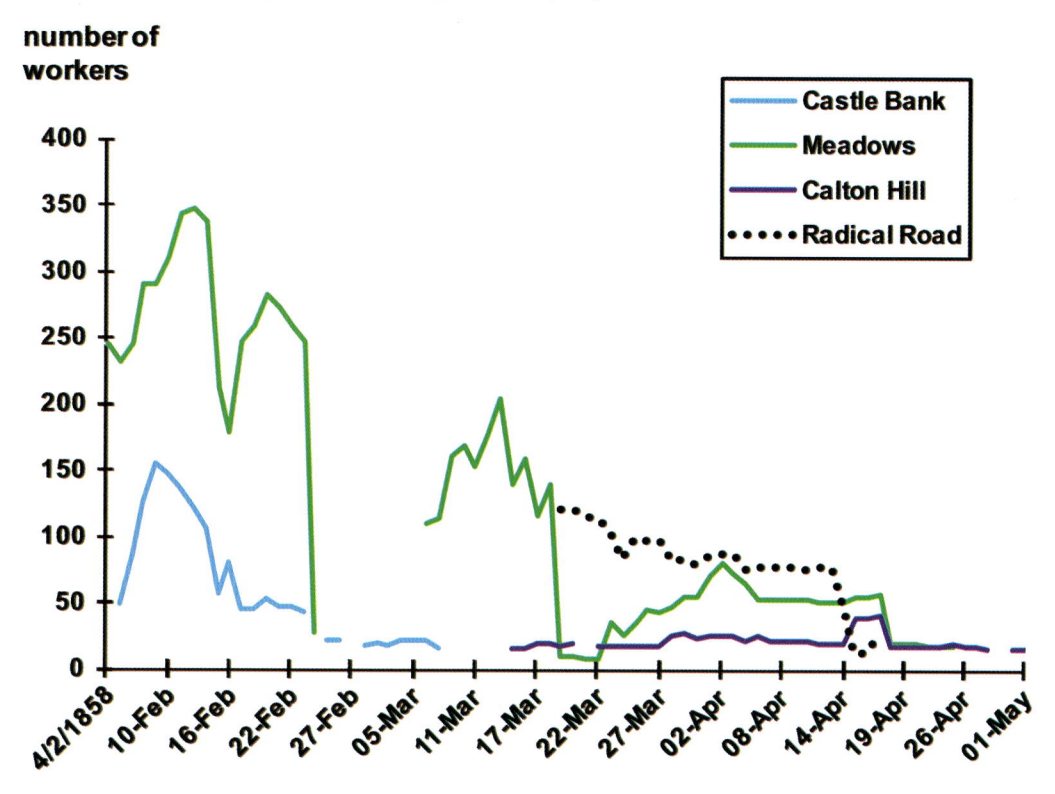

4.8 Stone-breaking and Paving: Unemployment Relief 1858

the architect. There was, obviously, a strong connection memorialising Thomas Chalmers (died 1847) with a Free Church and School alongside the housing; and the design, like Shaw Place, was a single continuous terrace block with entry from both sides. The socio-economic character had some similarities too. Gone were the marble workers and in their place were masons and joiners who together constituted one-third of all household heads in Chalmers Buildings; clerks were the second largest grouping. As a further indicator of the type of residents, there were two employers, both iron founders, who together employed 18 men and 9 boys.[24] Rents averaged approximately £7 p.a., well above the median rent in the city, and so beyond the reach of a multitude of labourers employed at Port Hopetoun and Port Hamilton in over twenty dockside timber, stone, and coal yards.

4.9 Chalmers Buildings dwarfed by the Exchange quarter
©John Reiach

PHOTO: John Reiach

Across the Union Canal from Chalmers Buildings, and opposite the graceful arc of Gardner's Crescent (1822), another worker's housing development 'built for the better class of mechanics' was already underway in 1853. Rosebank Cottages (Fig. 4.12) were planned, financed, and built by a railway contractor and builder, James Gowans who, unusually, also lived in his development at number 34 between 1855 and 1859.[25] *The Builder* explained the advantages of these 'cottages':

> '. . . first, a distinct and independent entrance; secondly a plot of ground for bleaching or for flowers; thirdly, a water-closet; fourthly, a scullery, with washing tubs, bath and hot-water; fifthly, a separate access to each apartment from the lobby, without going through an adjoining room, and sixthly, ample provision of ventilation and for warming small bed-rooms, which have no fireplaces.'[26]

The central spine of the development gave access to three rows of cottages, thirty-six in all, with gardens and a distinctive ironwork

4.10 Fountainbridge 1861 showing Chalmers, Rosemount and Rosebank Housing

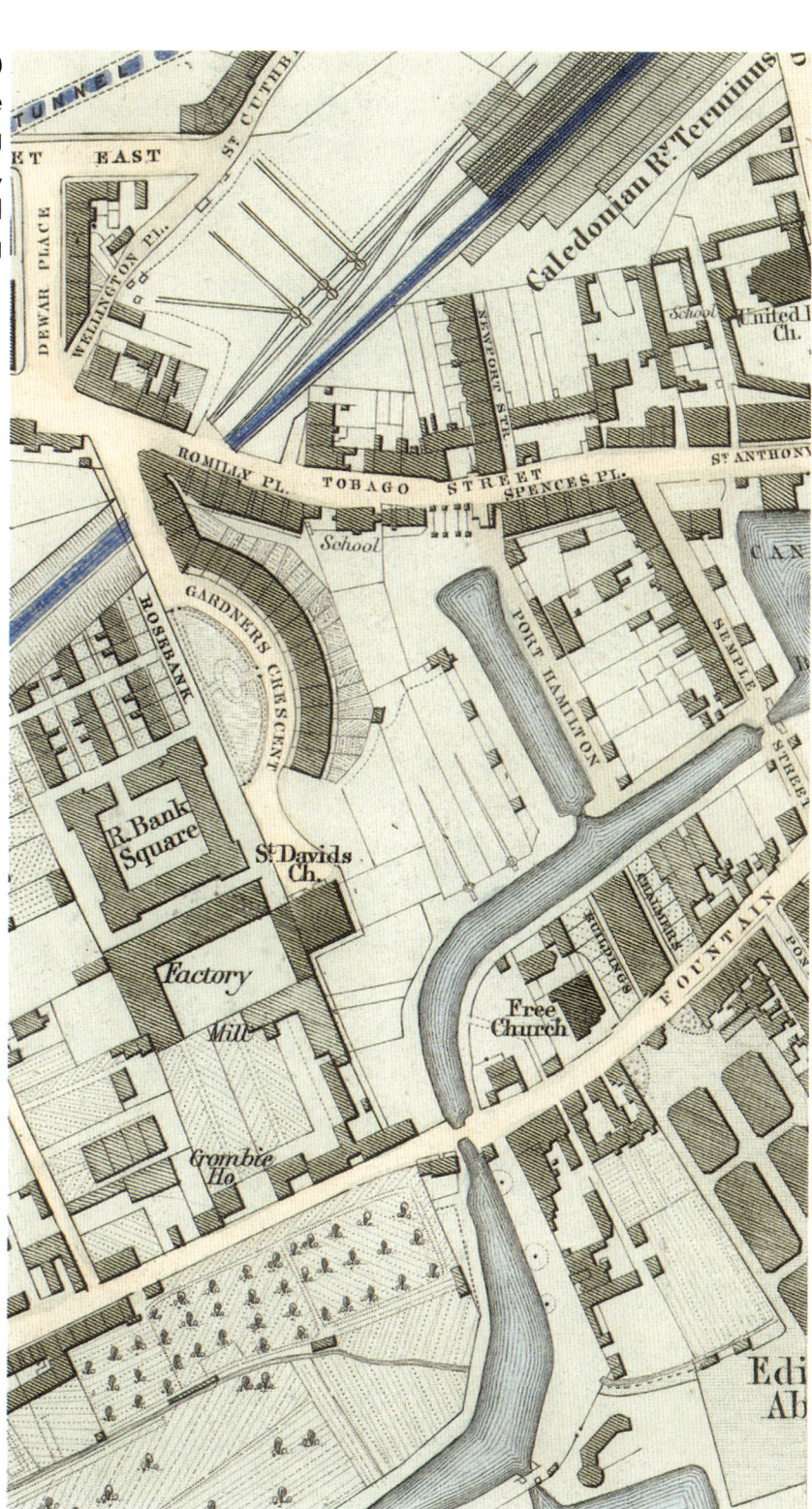

Source: Johnston's Map of Edinburgh and Leith 1861. © NLS

external staircase to the upper flats. *The Builder*'s correspondent thought these staircases 'no improvement' on conventional designs and regarded the cottages as 'two (sic) highly rented to be within the means of ordinary working people'.[27] If the spelling was doubtful, the reporter's observation was accurate. Rents averaged £14.50 – about a fifth (19%) above the level of labourers. Of 32 employed Rosebank household heads, legal and other clerks (7) paid an average rent of £14.90, and Inland Revenue officers (5) averaged £15.25. The diversity of employment was evident since there were another eighteen different occupations amongst household heads. Weekly rents were paid to Gowans' 51 year-old clerk, William Dobie, who moved in to number 34 Rosebank when Gowans moved out to his new home in Merchiston Park.[28]

Rosebank Cottages, a speculative development by Gowans who in 1861 remained the proprietor of all Rosebank homes, each cost between £160-£220, or between 20-80% more than early Stockbridge Colony houses. There is no justification, therefore, for considering Rosebank as 'an experiment in social housing' as has been claimed.[29] In terms of design, however, the Rosebank development possessed a feature that became the trademark of the Edinburgh Cooperative Building Company's – an external staircase entry to upper flats.

Rosemount Buildings was, and is, a distinctive red and yellow three-storey brick-built block of 96 homes around an extensive inner court or quadrangle. It was one of the first brick construction residential buildings in Edinburgh, and an initiative in 1859 of James Walker, self-described in the Census as an advocate and landed proprietor, resident at 42 Heriot Row. By the spring of 1861 all 96 properties of the Rosemount Building Association were occupied and home to 400 souls. Like Rosebank, there was considerable diversity in the type of work male residents undertook: indeed, there were 63 different occupations amongst the 129 resident males aged over 13. After clerks and joiners (both 10), railway employees (9), masons (7) there was a long list of unique occupations amongst Rosemount residents. Unusually, there was a cluster of five residents employed as 'electric telegraph' workers in what *The Scotsman* described as 'Intramural Telegraphy'.[30] These operatives managed a telegraph wire running from the Princes Street shop of cabinetmakers John Taylor & Son to masts at Charlotte Street, Rutland Street, Romilly Place and the firm's Rosemount works.

4.11 James Gowans (1821-90)
Source: *The Bailie*, vol. XXVIII, no.722, New series Vol.1, no.20 18 Aug. 1886. Reproduced with permission of University of Glasgow Archives & Special Collections: Bh12-d.1-30

Re-thinking the City

4.12 Rosebank Cottages and Rosemount Buildings
PHOTO: John Reiach

4.13 Rosemount inner courtyard
Source: John Reiach

47

Table 4.2 'New-Build' Housing for the Working Classes: Edinburgh 1850-65

name of buildings	location	date built	families (no.)	occupants (no.)	total cost (£)
		1	2	3	4
Pilrig Buildings	Shaw Street, Place	1850	62	203	6,800
Ashley Buildings	Trunk's Close/Leith Wynd	1851	70	178	5,100
Rosebank Cottages	Gardner's Crescent	1853	36	162	n/k
Chalmers Buildings	Fountainbridge	1855	29	135	3,600
Rosemount Buildings	Fountainbridge	1859	96	403	11,780
Begg's Buildings	Abbeyhill, Brand Place	1860	66	264	6,000
Milne's Buildings	Tron/North Bridge	1860	20	424	2,356
Croall's Buildings	Abbeyhill, Duncan Close	1860	30	80	3,600
Patriot Hall	Hamilton Place	1861	42	179	4,800
View Craig	Pleasance/St Leonard's St	1862	110	597	15,000
Prince Albert	Pleasance/St Leonard's St	1863	132	704	19,200
Blackwood's Buildings	Abbeyhill	1863	26	30	3,000
Prospect Street	Pleasance/St Leonard's St	1863	74	501	3,600
Gillis' Buildings	Nicolson Street	1863	12	n/k	1,800
Clermiston Buildings	Canongate/St Stephen's	1863	20	91	1,750
Rae's Buildings	Pleasance/St Leonard's St	1864	26	136	2,500
Gladstone's Buildings	Canongate	1864	32	n/k	2,000

What was perhaps surprising about Rosebank was that just 1.3% of household heads in 1861 were born in Edinburgh. In Rosemount Buildings it was 12%; Ashley Buildings, locally born household heads constituted 20% of the total, and in Begg's Buildings, 28%. Residents in Chalmers Buildings, where Free Church and Free Church School occupied contiguous plots to the housing, 37% of the tenants were born within the city of Edinburgh boundaries.[31] More surprising, perhaps, was the fact that of the first twenty shareholders in the Edinburgh Cooperative Building Company, *none* was born in Edinburgh. Were emigres from Selkirk to Shetland, Argyll to Angus more attuned to a cooperative enterprise and shareholding, albeit under the newly minted Limited Liability Act, 1855?[32] This legislation allowed limited liability companies with at least 25 shareholders to be held liable directly to creditors for a portion of their shares.

It seems that the 'lad o' pairts' drifted towards the capital and, with sufficient enterprise, skills, and persistence managed to secure a solid, low-rise, individual dwelling for himself and his family. It is

Re-thinking the City

av. cost (£) 5	lowest rent p.a(£) 6	rate of return (%) 7	Rooms	Closets	Kitchen	Water	Gas	Green/ Court	WC
110	5.60	5.11	1	–	1	1	1	1	1/3
73	3.60	4.94	1	1	1	1	1	1	1/3
220	n/k	n/k	2	1	1	1	–	1	1
124	7.00	5.64	1	1	1	1	1	1	1
123	7.00	n/k	1	1	1	1	1	1	1/2
91	6.50	7.15	1	2	1	1	1	1	1
118	8.50	7.22	1	1	1	1	1	1	1
120	5.25	4.38	1	–	1	1	1	1	1
114	9.75	8.53	2	–	1	1	1	1	1
136	7.25	5.32	1	1	1	1	1	–	1
145	9.50	6.65	1	1	1	1	1	1	1
115	7.35	6.37	1	1	1	1	1	1	1/2
49	3.00	6.17	1	–	1	1	1	1	1/5
150	10.00	6.67	1	1	–	1	1	–	1
88	7.00	8.00	2	–	1	1	1	1	1/2
96	6.30	6.55	1	–	1	1	1	1	1
63	3.00	4.80	1	–	1	1	1	1	–

likely that this life course also explains both the generally lower percentage of female heads of household in model dwellings, and the generally lower average age of adults. Overall, female heads of household accounted for 30% of all properties in the city in 1861. None of the early 'model' dwellings projects achieved this with Ashley Buildings 26.7% closest to the city average and the others considerably adrift: Rosemount 17%; Pilrig 14%; Rosebank 11%; Begg's 8%; and Chalmers 6%.[33]

Significantly, all but Ashley Buildings were urban 'fringe' developments. Their relationship to the city differed little from the subsequent Edinburgh Cooperative Building Company's sites. Indeed, these were 'plantation' or Colony settlements before 'The Colonies.' As 'new builds' with improved amenities they were in better condition than most of the existing housing stock in the Old Town, Canongate, West Port, Water of Leith and the inappropriately named Pleasance. The lowest rentals in each location (Table 4.2, col. 6) also reflected this with the centrally located Ashley Buildings significantly cheaper than the later fringe developments. Without

Source: H. D. Littlejohn, *Report on the Sanitary Condition of Edinburgh* (Edinburgh 1865), p.39, facsimile reprinted in P. Laxton and R. Rodger, *Insanitary City*; NRS, VR100/ 33-37

49

4.14 Begg's Buildings, Abbeyhill

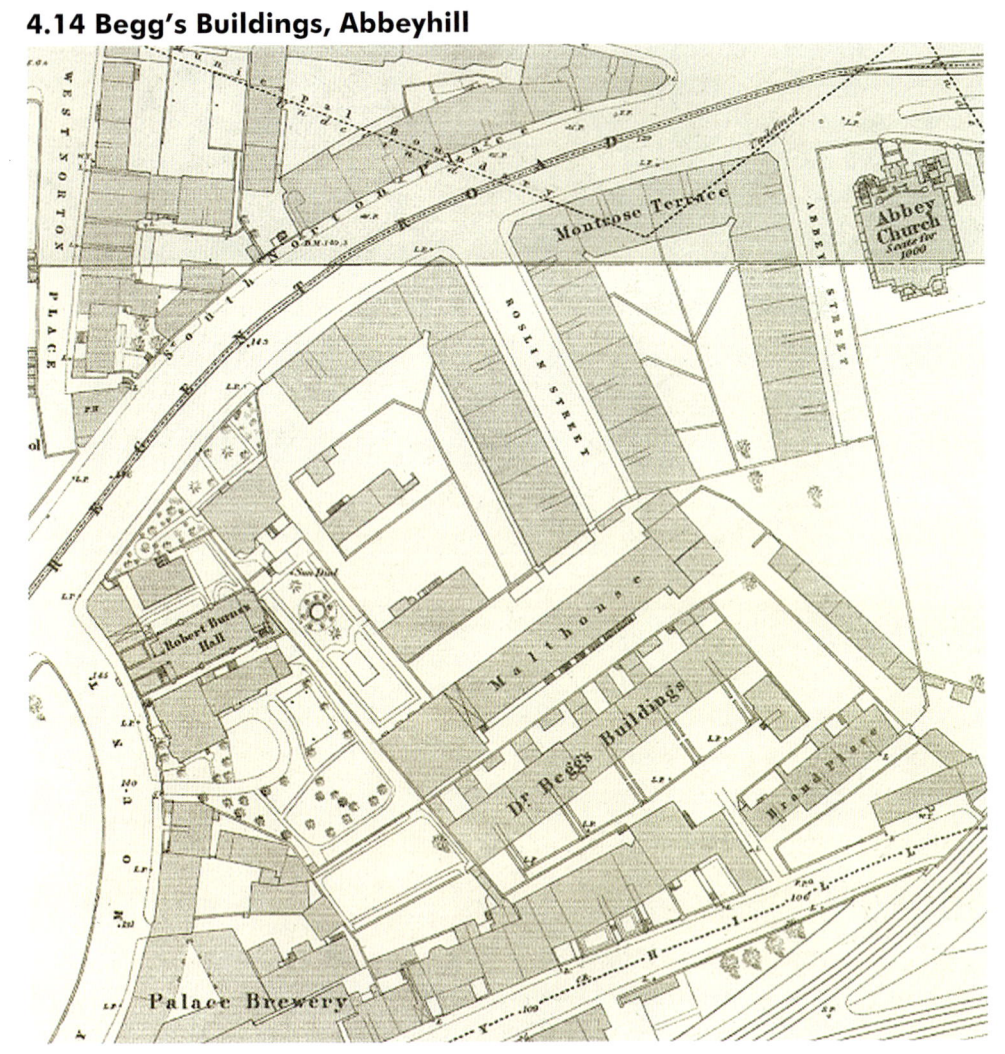

Source: Reproduced with the permission of the NLS OS large scale town plan, 1849-53

new plantation housing pressure on Old Town tenement stock would have been even greater.

Almost invariably, commercial considerations influenced the rental levels in the early 'model' dwellings and Edinburgh developments generally obtained a rate of return on capital in the 5-7% range (Table 4.2, col. 7). Indeed, the phrase 'Five Per Cent philanthropy' became synonymous with model dwellings.[34] Often a prominent individual or developer was involved. For example, Mr Matheson was the promoter for Chalmers Buildings; nearby, James Walker, advocate, invested in Rosemount Buildings. Milne's Buildings took the name of their sponsor, a brassfounder, and the three-storeyed balcony access to Patriot Hall flats were the building

4.15 Upper and Lower View Craig Row, St Leonard's

Source: Capital Collections ECL negative A907B

project of J. A. Cheyne, and subsequently his trustees. James Gowans initiated thirty-six Rosebank 'flatted cottages' for 'the better class of mechanics' and remained the proprietor of the entire development into the early 1860s.

Some 'capitalists' who financed artisan housing no doubt had a social conscience; others had an eye for a market opportunity for housing skilled workers. With Dr Begg's Buildings at Brand Place, Abbeyhill, surrounded by breweries, it was not Begg at all but another wealthy investor, Robert Cranston, son of a mason and owner of the Waverley Temperance Hotel on Princes Street, who advanced the £6,000 capital for the construction of 72 new homes for 226 individuals. The investment, managed by Macqueen & Bridgeford, solicitors at 72 Princes Street, produced a net annual rental in 1861 of £479 – average rent £6.65 – which on an investment of £6,000 was equivalent to an 8% return over 12.5 years.[35] This was a substantially better result than government stocks in 1860-61 (average 5.0%), and though the uncertainty associated with the American Civil War did push rates up over 7% in 1863-64, the interest rate generally was around the 3-4% over the course of a twelve year investment.[36]

Despite the level of investment, one-third of 'Beggies' still lived in households of six or more members, and normally in a single

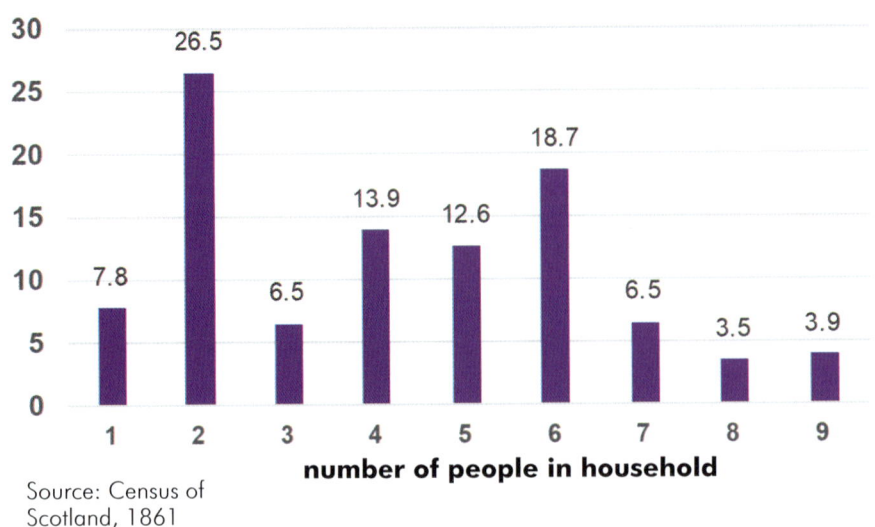

4.16 Household Size: Begg's Buildings, Brand Place 1861 (%)

number of people in household	%
1	7.8
2	26.5
3	6.5
4	13.9
5	12.6
6	18.7
7	6.5
8	3.5
9	3.9

Source: Census of Scotland, 1861

room. 'Model' housing was extolled as rescuing or restoring moral and physical well-being to the occupants as well as providing business models that appealed to capitalists. On a case-by-case basis this was probably a fair assessment, but on a city-wide basis was wide of the mark. What Rev Dr James Begg had identified, however, not without significance for the future Edinburgh Cooperative Building Company, was the importance of access to land for building workers' homes. He explained:

> 'There does not seem any reason why, around every increasing town, a portion of land ought not to be scheduled out by Act of Parliament, as in the case of railways, to be taken, if desired, under the supervision of the competent authorities at a fair price, as sites for suitable trades-men's houses.
>
> Source: *The Scotsman*, 31 May, 1860, p.2.

Land became the perennial problem of the ECBC – and ultimately defined its success.

The nature of the 'housing problem', both nationally and in Edinburgh, could not be better represented than through these model housing initiatives. To build for the skilled working class was financially viable for the developer and landlord but did little to address the shortfall of affordable housing supply for workers – the labourers and casually employed. Lacking regular incomes these tenants were obliged to rent out sub-divided flats in existing often

Table 4.3 Typical Tenements: Scot's Land, 341 Cowgate

	rooms	families	children under 5	adults	total	sinks	water closets
First Floor	9	8	8	25	33	—	—
Second Floor	11	8	4	22	26	—	—
Third Floor	11	8	10	24	34	—	—
Fourth Floor	10	7	8	26	34	—	—
Fifth Floor	7	6	6	216	22	—	—
Back Land	5	5	6	15	21	—	—
total	53	42	42	128	170	—	—

Source: H. D. Littlejohn, *Report on the Sanitary Condition of the City of Edinburgh*, p.32.

dilapidated and insanitary tenements, scattered throughout the Old Town, and increasingly at some distance from the workplace. Landlords also sub-divided their properties to ensure their flats were affordable and to avoid the landlord's curse – vacancies! The resulting overcrowding was prejudicial to health and so compromised continuity to workers' employment. The lodging house or the sub-divided room became the back-stop form of accommodation.

Thus the urban environment became particularly hostile for a considerable number of Edinburgh residents, with a culture of endemic poverty alleviated occasionally by churches and charities, such as the Edinburgh City Mission and, after 1868, The Edinburgh Association for Improving the Condition of the Poor.[37] A crisp *Scotsman* editorial in 1860 captured the nature of supply and demand in the housing market and prophetically suggested that 'if a proper return for capital can be realised' then the possibility of a joint-stock company called 'The Edinburgh Association for Building Houses for the Working Classes' could succeed.[38]

Happy Homes

PHOTO: John Reiach

Dalry Colonies pathway

5. A Change of Tone

INTERCONNECTED factors in the 1850s combined to change attitudes that contributed in 1861 to the formation of the Edinburgh Cooperative Building Company and the foundation stone ceremony. What linked them all was press coverage, specifically *The Scotsman*, *Edinburgh Courant*, and the Free Church's *The Witness*, each of which engaged in a practical way with various physical and psychological issues surrounding housing conditions. Sometimes sensationalism was necessary to shock the complacent citizenry.

At one level newspaper coverage was coloured by moral outrage and outright panic. *The Scotsman* conducted an extended investigation in February 1850 into daily life and housing conditions in the West Port. What agitated correspondents most was that 'the influences of religion and the refinement, and even the civilisation of Edinburgh, is about as little felt as it is in the centre of Africa'.[1] Because 'the different classes live and die without knowledge of each other', the fear of the crowd or, as *The Scotsman* put it, 'a multitude of squalid figures and wild faces', might cause a 'commotion' and so 'break up the existence of order in Edinburgh . . . which, if not of revolutionary violence, at any rate in terrific appearance, would not be surpassed by the mass of classes dangereuses in any city in all Europe'.[2] Had the revolutions of 1848 in Europe reached Edinburgh in 1850?

Inflammatory language was used by *The Scotsman*'s 'Special Commissioner', James Bruce, to describe the 'dangerous classes' as 'the whole of the classes who work occasionally as "labourers"' and for whom it was not possible to be indolent and not criminal.'[3] The *Edinburgh News* subsequently contributed to this moral panic by describing Old Town houses as 'chambers of death' and scapegoating the residents as 'constitutional drunkards'.[4] To substantiate the claim the newspaper instanced the immoral and disorderly behaviour of three girls in a Leith Wynd flat. Each had consumed a gill of whisky and, while 'painting her face', one remarked, 'what's the use of a shop without a sign?' The account concluded:

> 'Destitution, prostitution and crime in Edinburgh may be said to hold high levee on Saturday night. . . and from seven till twelve o'clock is the best time to see the orgy. Congregated on either side of the North Bridge . . . may be seen (the most) disgusting sights possible to conjure up, even in the imagination of those novelists who take strange delight in pouring out scenes.'
> Source: R. Foulis, *Old Houses in Edinburgh and their Inhabitants* (1852)

For those without detailed personal knowledge of life in the closes and wynds descriptive passages of orgy and immorality by journalists provided salacious descriptions. It was Bruce who in plain language exposed the acute social and environmental inequalities and correspondingly unhealthy living conditions within the poorest parts of the city:

> '. . . within bow-shot of the splendid mansions of a population boasting themselves to be possessed of a purity in religious knowledge and practice unexampled amongst Christian nations, a kingdom of darkness, misery, and vice, has erected itself, and is daily strengthening its fortifications and deepening its trenches.'
> Source: Inquiry in Destitution and Vice in Edinburgh, *The Scotsman*, 2 Feb 1850, col 2a

The counter narrative, also presented in press coverage, was the visible success of new housing projects for workmen and their families. Pilrig, Ashley, Chalmers and other workmen's building projects in the 1850s were reported in positive language. Important in this regard was the contribution of Hugh Miller, a Cromarty stonemason who had worked in a Niddrie masons' sheds, contracted pneumoconiosis, and after a short interval was recruited in 1840 as founding editor and later proprietor of *The Witness* – the bi-weekly Free Church publication which by the 1850s had the highest newspaper circulation in Edinburgh.[5] Hugh Miller, described as 'a brilliant journalist' with a vigorous and controversial style, wrote about 10,000 words each week from 1840 to 1856 attacking prominent individuals and explaining poverty not in terms of indolence but as the result of the practices and powers of a propertied class. He observed: 'We must devise some plan by which proper buildings shall be erected, and insure the future well-being of the people'.[6] In this respect Miller echoed James Begg's speech in 1850 on the issues of housing and health to the founding meeting of the Scottish Social Reform Association: 'You will never get the unclean heart of Edinburgh gutted out until you plant it all round with new houses'.[7] The concept of 'Colony' housing and plantations was already apparent.

Similarly, Hugh Gilzean-Reid (1836-1911) with his Free Kirk background and newspaper experience in Aberdeenshire, moved south and used his position as Editor with the *Edinburgh Weekly News* and the *Scottish Press* (1859-63) to support Edinburgh stonemasons in their long dispute with their employers. Reid's vigorous style and frequent public speaking appearances in support of the strikers were managed – and toned down – by his wife, Anne, who later became president of the Women's Liberal Association.[8] In his spell of just four years in Edinburgh, Reid was deeply committed to the issues of greater independence for working men. It was hardly surprising given their written and oratorical impact and undoubted name recognition locally that this was then perpetuated in the street names of the first two 'Colony' housing developments, Reid Terrace and Hugh Miller Place.

If newspaper articles detailed specific housing concerns, three internationally renowned published works in 1859 – *Origin of Species*, *Self-Help*, and *On Liberty* – from authors each with Edinburgh connections provided a more detached justification to seek alternative approaches to housing provision and happy homes. Charles Darwin's interest in natural history and his path-breaking *Origin of Species* (1859) was partly a result of his disenchantment with medical education at Edinburgh University (1825-31). Central themes of Darwin's book, 'natural selection' and evolutionary biology, were implicit in local writing about degeneracy amongst an illiterate and irreligious class in Edinburgh. Pamphlets and letter columns contained a constant flow of correspondence about the morals and behaviour of the poor and expressed long run concern about mutations in the human species. *Classes dangereuses* was not just about riots and anti-social behaviour but about genetics. Again in 1859 and with Edinburgh connections, the journalist Samuel Smiles published

5.1 Hugh Gilzean Reid (1836-1911)

Oil on Canvas, Hal Hurst 1900. Courtesy University of Aberdeen ABDUA 30070

5.2 Hugh Miller (1802-56)

Source: Bell-Wellcome L0012622

Self-Help.[9] It, too, addressed the behaviour of the poor who, through a lack of education were considered unable to participate in upward mobility in social or economic terms, and were in effect categorised as 'deserving' (of assistance) and 'undeserving' poor. John Stuart Mill's *On Liberty* claimed freedom of action and speech were central elements of a civilised society and important counters to the tyranny of government. The lengthy and sometimes dense arguments of all three authors probably reached few readers in crowded tenements but the general tone of self-help, self-control and self-esteem were worked through in relation to employment and urban environmental conditions following their publication in 1859.

An important change of tone was also evident at governmental level. The Industrial and Provident Societies Partnership Act, 1852 defined the future course of mutual and friendly societies.[10] It provided a legal framework for cooperatives by offering both a measure of protection for a mutual society's funds, and authorisation for profit-sharing with members capped at one-third of its profits. This was followed by the Limited Liability Act, 1855 which provided further reassurances, indeed limitations, to small businesses and organisations regarding the extent of their exposure to debts.[11]

6. Building Cooperation

THOUGH the Rochdale Society of Equitable Pioneers, established 1844, occupies an exalted place in cooperative history there were several earlier Scottish consumer cooperatives that pointed a way forward. These focussed initially on food – Victualling Societies – and were established in many Scottish burghs including Govan, Galashiels and Hawick.[1] Such mutual organisations were encouraged by the Free Church since they were based on self-help and thus combined a minimum of public involvement with a maximum of voluntary cooperation. Implicitly these organisations embraced the elements the *Origin of Species*, *Self-Help*, and *On Liberty*.

Cabinetmakers, blacksmiths and foundry workers had congregated in sufficient numbers mid-century around the Union Canal basins and Fountainbridge to discover a degree of shared cultural solidarity based on work practices. A number of them formed a Committee of the Working Classes in 1858, convened a public meeting at the Buccleuch Street Hall on 15 July 1858, and published a Report compiled by ten working men to express their views 'on the overcrowded and uncomfortable state of their dwelling-houses'.[2] Such events, as with the Brighton Street Chapel meeting two months later, reinforced the group and class identity by re-stating the case against tenement owners who:

> 'pile storey upon storey, until the wall sometimes cracked and tottered under the superincumbent weight. . . evil consequences of this were. . . nothing more than towers of dark cellars saturated with garbage; and within their dingy precincts children were said to have rotted like sheep.'
>
> Source: Report, p.10

6.1 Title page of A. Macpherson, *Report of the Committee of the Working Classes of Edinburgh on the Present Overcrowded and Uncomfortable State of their Dwelling Houses* (Edinburgh 1860)

The decision to form a cooperative society was taken after yet another public meeting, on this occasion in the Thornybauk Schoolroom (Fountainbridge) in August 1859. A month later a committee had been appointed, rules established, official joint stock limited liability company registration submitted, and fifty members recruited. A corner shop site was obtained at 50 (now 97) Fountainbridge and Ponton Street near the Union Canal basin and Chalmers Buildings which opened for business on 4 November 1859. The decision to establish St Cuthbert's Cooperative Association owed much, firstly, to the industrial recession and social unrest that surfaced in 1859; secondly, to inspiration drawn from the activities of skilled men in the north of England, west of Scotland, and from the energy of the Edinburgh Trades Council members; and thirdly, from a wish to side-step the profiteering and money-lending practices of shopkeepers by selling goods directly to a membership that benefitted from both lower prices and what was an early form of a loyalty card – the 'divi'(dend).

The cooperative principle obtained further exposure when the publisher William Chambers intervened with a powerful lecture

6.2 Co-operative Society Branches: Edinburgh and Leith, 1859-1910

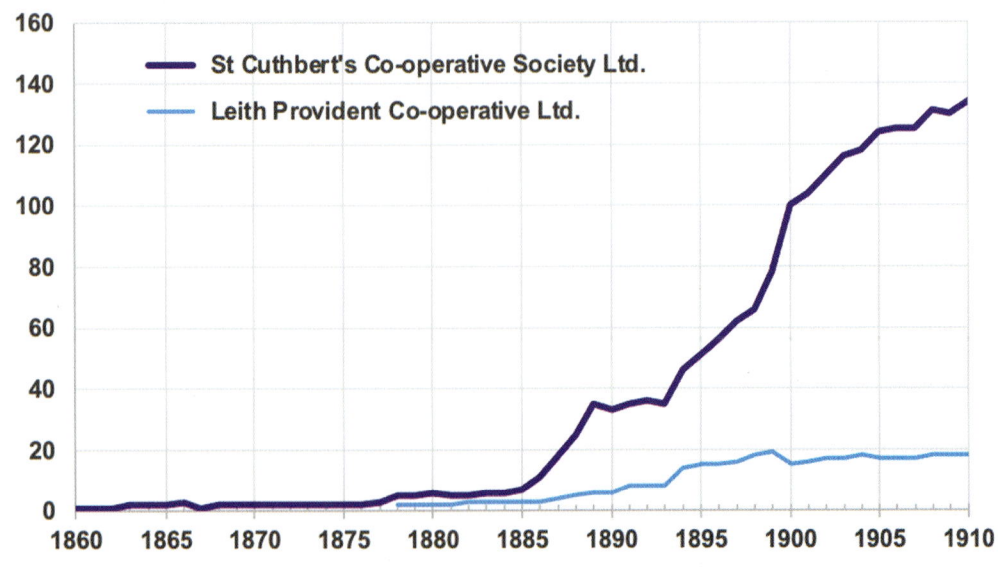

Source: Edinburgh and Leith Post Office Directories 1855-1915

on the subject in 1860, later printed and widely distributed.³ Other cooperative companies with a local emphasis followed St Cuthbert's lead: St Margaret's Cooperative Society (Abbey); Edinburgh Cooperative Society (Richmond Place); Greenside Cooperative Society (Union Place); Water of Leith Cooperative Society (Dean Path); and the Western Cooperative Society (Grove Street). None, however, survived their initial problems. The first few years were also particularly difficult for St Cuthbert's Cooperative which functioned on a very modest scale (Fig.6.2). Even several years after its foundation the Registrar of Friendly Societies, placed St Cuthbert's only 55th of 126 cooperative societies in Scotland – far behind Kilmarnock (14 times that of St Cuthbert's turnover) or Brechin and Blairgowrie (both 10 times greater), and just ahead of little Bonnyrigg in terms of its scale of business. While St Cuthbert's Cooperative Society was founded earlier, it functioned with only a single outlet at Ponton street, and briefly, a Brunswick Street branch in the 1860s, in contrast to the ECBC which sold nearly 500 homes in the same decade.⁴

6.3 Amalgamated Carpenters and Joiners of Scotland: Blue Blanket

Source: Edinburgh City Museums

Edinburgh had its own cooperative pioneers. Out of concern for working conditions, a few tradesmen activists established the Edinburgh Trades Council in 1853 – the first place after Liverpool to do so.⁵ This federated body acted on behalf of the shared interests of several artisanal trades. Prominent in the organisation were James G. Bald (plumbers), John Borrowman and William Caw (carpenters and joiners) and the specific issues that energised them was their request for a Saturday half day, and the payment of wages on a Friday rather than a Saturday.⁶ The Trades Council initiated a publicity campaign in 1859 designed to extend its membership by ordering 'a circular be printed urging upon working men the necessity of supporting this association so as to enable us to carry out any important object that we may take up'.⁷ Whereas a Convenery of Trades had provided a collective presence in the city for the 'freemen masters' and burgesses since 1562, three hundred years later a Trades Council represented the interests of labour.⁸

6.4 Memorandum of Association, ECBC 4 July 1861

We, the several persons whose Names and Addresses are Subscribed are desirous of being formed into a Company, in pursuance of this Memorandum of Association; and we respectively agree to take the Number of Shares in the Capital of the Company set opposite our respective Names.—

	Names and Addresses of Subscribers.	No. of Shares taken by each Subscriber.	
1.	David Rintoul Mason, of Edinburgh, in the County of Edinburgh	5	£5.
2.	John Ogilvie Mason, of Edinburgh, in the County of Edinburgh	5	£5.
3.	James Collins Mason, of Edinburgh, in the County of Edinburgh	1	£1.
4.	William Mill Mason, of Edinburgh, in the County of Edinburgh	5	£5.
5.	Thomas Morgan Mason, of Edinburgh, in the County of Edinburgh	3	£3.
6.	James Carshman Mason, of Edinburgh, in the County of Edinburgh	1	£1.
7.	John W. Lyvele Mason, of Edinburgh, in the County of Edinburgh	5	£5.
	Total Shares taken and their Value	25	£25.

Dated the Twenty Eighth day of June One Thousand Eight Hundred and Sixty one.—

Witness to the above signatures.
John Paterson, Solicitor, 56. George Street, Edinburgh.

The Edinburgh Co-operative Building Company Limited is incorporated pursuant to the Joint Stock Companies Acts 1856 & 1857 this Fourth day of July, Eighteen Hundred and Sixty one.—

John Henderson
Registrar Joint Stock Companies
Scotland.

Source: NRS BT2/1970/548 See also J. Begg, *Happy Homes for Working Men*, 1866 edn., pp.71-105.

Bitter industrial relations characterised the year 1859. Employers in the London building trades locked out over 24,000 workers after masons went on strike demanding a nine-hour day. The dispute, considered by the Edinburgh Trades Council 'as a seminal event in British trade union history', spilled over locally into 1860.[9] *The Scotsman* presented it as a moral dilemma: should union funds intended for relief of the infirm and aged be used to support strikers, especially as higher death rates occurred amongst strikers' families?[10]

Moral support for the workers' position, however, was forthcoming locally and from a variety of influential national figures. Notable amongst them were Richard Cobden (Rochdale MP) and John Bright (Rochdale-born, MP for Manchester, then Birmingham) who were founders of the Anti-Corn Law League which sought to remove taxes on grain and thus reduce the cost of food for all, and especially for the poor.[11] Cobden and Bright also supported electoral reform, religious freedom, and the Freehold Land Movement which aimed to reduce taxes on land and so reduce housing costs. John Bright had a particularly strong personal friendship and collaboration with Duncan McLaren (Edinburgh Lord Provost 1851-54, and MP 1861-85) who after 6 July 1848 was his brother-in-law when McLaren married Bright's sister, Priscilla, in Rochdale Registrar's Office. This active, reformist network included McLaren's colleague in the Freehold Movement in the 1850s, Rev Dr James Begg, who in turn acknowledged the 'commanding ability' of Duncan McLaren, and the contributions of William Chambers and Dr Henry Littlejohn, Medical Officer of Health for the City.[12] What was significant, therefore, was that powerful individuals had moved away from evangelical injunctions to improve moral behaviour of the poor; social control measures were in retreat. Instead, mutual help was in the process of replacing self-help.

In terms of the strike itself, the stakes in Edinburgh were raised after George Potter, President of the London Trades Council and a key figure in the London building strike, gave a lecture on 20 February 1861 at the Brighton Street Chapel attended by over 2,000 persons. Afterwards, the Edinburgh Trades Council pledged 'to use all legal means to establish nine hours as a day's work instead of ten as at present' and their leading officials, John Borrowman and William Caw, central figures also in the foundation of St Cuthbert's Cooperative Society, were again instrumental. They established a union – the Amalgamated Society of Carpenters and Joiners of Scotland – following another packed meeting in Buccleuch Street Hall in March 1861. Vocal support for workers was also forthcoming from Free Church ministers, notably Rev Dr James Begg, and in print from Hugh Gilzean Reid and his fellow editors and journalists.[13]

For three months in the spring of 1861 over 1,300 Edinburgh masons and joiners were denied access to building sites. Employers called it a 'strike'; to workers it was a 'lock out'. *The Scotsman* described it as 'a renewal of the disastrous builders' strike in London' in 1859.[14] Newspaper articles and the letters columns posed union power contesting managerial autonomy. The language of class, then, was at the heart of the dispute. Some observers even claimed that the middle class worked harder than the working class, an argument countered by columnists who claimed that in Edinburgh, as elsewhere, because of the tracts and newspapers they read and lectures they attended, there was 'a portion of the working-men, the mechanics and tradesmen, better informed than the middle classes of society'.[15] Whether strike or lock-out, approximately 860 masons lost their jobs, 260 left Edinburgh to seek employment elsewhere, and joiners were forced back to work for lack of Union funds. Some employers of 'large squads' conceded to the demands and others, in a more conciliatory mood, offered a 51-hour week instead of 57 hours. Another group of employers, provocatively, formed their own association and explored the potential for machine-dressed stone cutting to counter the power of labour.

However, even before the lock-out was over, and with 200 stonemasons still on strike, an attempt was made by building trades workers to manage their own employment conditions and housing prospects.[16] Stonemasons took an extraordinary initiative. They decided on 17 April 1861 at the Mason's Hall, Lyon's Close to form a limited liability company, the Edinburgh Cooperative Building Company Limited, with a total capital of £10,000. Their registration number SC000079 indicates that the ECBC was just the 79th limited liability company in Scotland. It was a truly path-breaking development. The Memorandum of Association (Fig 6.4) stated that:

> The objects for which the Company is established are the carrying on the business of Building in all its branches, including Joiner-work as well as Mason-work, and in every other work incidental or conducive to the business of Building in all its branches, and that either by Contract or Speculation; including the acquisition, either by Purchase, Lease, or other tenure, of House Property and of Land, for the purpose of erecting thereon Houses and other Buildings.
> Source: NRS, BT2/1970/548/79/1, Edinburgh Building Contractors, Ltd.; Memorandum of Association, Edinburgh Cooperative Building Company 1861

Why, then, did a group of Edinburgh stonemasons embark on their cooperative odyssey? What made them suppose that they might succeed where others failed? There were several factors that persuaded stonemasons to take this course of action which had nothing to do with the collapsed tenement at 99-103 High Street and 35 fatalities which occurred seven months *later* on 24 November 1861.[17] Uppermost, firstly, was the stonemasons' sense of frustration with employers. The lock-out in 1861 demonstrated how dependent workers were on employers not just for work, but through their pay packets for the standard of housing they could afford. Secondly, the quality of affordable accommodation seriously impaired the quality of life and shortened it. This was increasingly evident from the mortality data collected in the 1850s. Thirdly, there was encouragement and support from prominent church figures and newspaper editors which induced a greater degree of self-confidence amongst working men, as in northern England. As the Free Church later put it: 'What English men have done to a large extent in the erection of thousands of houses, Scotchmen can do'.[18] The cooperative credentials and political momentum were both positive factors in the stonemasons' initiative, and the architectural press and knowledgeable housing reformers endorsed a radical approach to workers' housing. Connected with this, fourthly, was the introduction in 1855 of limited liability which put a ceiling on the financial losses that workmen might incur.

Fifthly, and crucially, the Edinburgh economy was on the point of a period of expansion. This had been identified by working men and reported in surveys of several Edinburgh tradesmen in 1858 who, significantly, commented on the migration of workshops and factories to the fringes of the city.[19] The general economic expansion was evident in the development of railway depots, handling and warehousing facilities on the western (Haymarket/Dalry) and eastern (Abbeyhill) edges of Edinburgh to produce a shift in the location and scale of industry from the late-1850s.[20] Centrally, too, the south and back Canongate plots were colonised by workshops. More specifically, Fountainbridge experienced major physical changes and employment opportunities with the arrival of new slaughterhouses, William McEwan's brewery, North British Rubber Mills, the ironfounders Thomas Robb and J. Learmonth and Co., and nearby, the Caledonian Distillery with its distinctive chimney, still standing, near Dalry Road. Few workers were better placed to understand this spatial change in the city economy than building tradesmen.

The activities of the ECBC can be considered through different lenses. Were their self-build cooperative intentions the product of a social system in disequilibrium? Or were ECBC aspirations more akin to those of the middle classes, in which case were the ECBC founders compliant, and so seeking to be consensual rather than conflictual, as is sometimes proposed by studies of labour history? Were the shared values of mutuality and corporate structures elements that contributed positively to social cohesion in the city? Was the ECBC itself an actor, shaping rather than adapting to an emerging social identity in the city. Or was the ECBC 'reflexive', that is, constructing its own identity and not simply cloned on existing values. The activities of the ECBC are now analysed with some of these different perspectives in mind.[21]

Building Cooperation

Dalry Colonies

PHOTO: John Reiach

Happy Homes

PHOTO: John Reiach

'Gabriel's ladder' connecting the colonies to the New Town via a staircase to Saxe Coburg Place

7. Structural Strength

THREE months after its formation in April 1861, the rules of the ECBC had been drafted, revised, and a thousand copies printed. By early July 1861, ground at Water Lane (now Glenogle Road) owned by the distiller James Haig had been viewed and, after some legal complications, feued on 23 August at £18 per acre per annum. The Company leased ground at Torphichen Street as an office and building yard. Quarry-masters were initially 'aloof' about the supply of stone to the ECBC until Councillor James Gowans 'came to the rescue'.[1] On 4 October 1861 the decision was taken to commence building. The foundation stone was laid on the 23 October, and by early November scaffolding was in place at Reid Terrace. In the next twenty years the ECBC acquired and developed ground at the rate of 2 acres per annum, sold over 1200 houses, and issued an average annual dividend of 10.3%.[2]

To publicise the ECBC and the principle of cooperation, a public meeting was convened in November 1861 in the Brighton Street Chapel, directly behind the site where Prince Albert had laid the foundation stone of the Scottish Industrial Museum in Chambers Street a month previously. The meeting was chaired by William Chambers, publisher, author on housing issues and five years later Lord Provost elected on a proactive reform platform to drive new streets through the insanitary housing of central Edinburgh.[3] He stressed that the meeting 'bore no political or sectarian complexion' and had 'no reference to any question between employers and employed'. Rather, Chambers explained, 'the scheme of cooperation that will be brought forward tonight is . . . calculated to promote that spirit of self-reliance and self-respect which we should all like to see cultivated'.[4]

Though the thirty-four Articles of Association made no explicit reference to the ECBC as an instrument by which workers would re-position themselves in the social order, three innovative clauses provided a basis by which they might do so. Clause 7 preserved a measure of control over decision-making for workers by stating: 'That the chairman, one of the vice-presidents, and at least eight of the ordinary directors, shall be building operatives'. In a complex and highly specific formulation, Clause 9 discriminated positively in favour of small shareholders by attaching a greater weight to their votes compared to large shareholders (Fig.7.1). And, with an exceptional awareness of gender issues, Clause 32 assured women of equal treatment within the organisation of the company by stating that 'notwithstanding any form of expression used herein, the whole conditions hereof shall be binding on females equally as well as male partners'.[5]

The transparent nature of the ECBC's administration was established from the outset. Monthly business meetings, quarterly general meetings, an annual meeting, elections by majority voting, and mechanisms for individuals and groups to convene extraordinary meetings in the event of losses sustained by the company – each demonstrated an unusual degree of participation and accountability through a code of governance. Once the Company was underway, even in the matter of house design, the directors agreed to a proposal at a general meeting that there should be a competition and cash prize of 2 guineas (£2.10 or the equivalent of about 35 hours work) for residents, shareholders

7.1 ECBC Voting Weighted in Favour of Small Shareholders

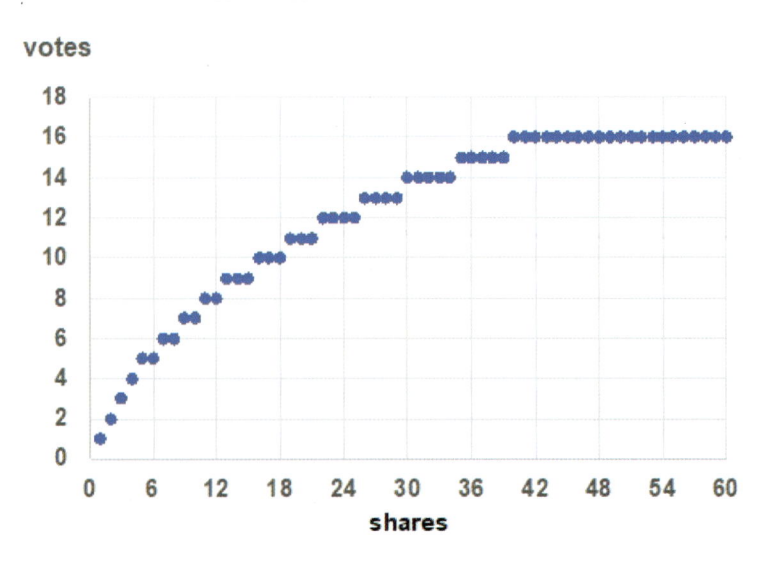

Source: N, GS27/505/1 and /2.

Structural Strength

7.2 Stockbridge Site: Edinburgh Cooperative Building Company, 1861

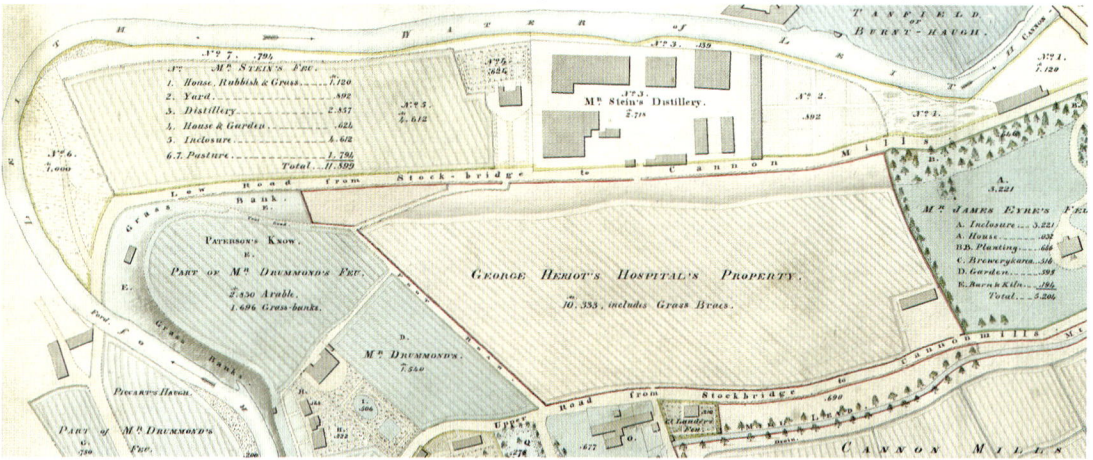

Source: reproduced with the permission of National Library of Scotland

7.3 Stockbridge aerial view

Source: Historic Environment Scotland

and workmen who presented designs or made practical suggestions for building. A management pattern was established with a Company office in Cockburn Street, open on Fridays for issuing shares and general business, and the Directors met on Tuesdays and Saturdays to discuss these and other company matters.[6]

The Memorandum of Association stated that when fully paid up the capital of the ECBC was £10,000 in £1 shares to which subscriptions could be paid in instalments of 5 shillings (0.25p). After only three days the Directors had issued 114 shares; within a week, 70 building trades workers, mostly stonemasons, had bought 160 shares, and the following week 42 shares were issued. Thereafter the subscriptions tapered off to give cause for concern to the Directors, whom James Begg described as 'brave men' who 'persevered gallantly.'[7] However, they held their nerve and by its first anniversary the ECBC had 341 registered shareholders, 41% of whom were stonemasons with other building trades accounting for a further 9%. Trade Associations were also active: the Cooperative Plasterers' Society bought fifty shares and the Operative Plumbers' Society took twenty.

In the aftermath of strike action, solidarity for the cooperative spirit was forthcoming from individuals in 55 other trades, and there were instances of several subscribers from within the same tenement. Seven shareholders gave a Bedford Street address, nine lived in Bristo Street, and there were a dozen subscribers living along Fountainbridge. Almost three in five (58%) of subscribers came from the Old Town and adjacent densely packed streets in the Pleasance, Causewayside and at Fountainbridge – the heart of the Cooperative movement in Edinburgh. A dozen of the original ECBC shareholders lived there and altogether 14% lived in adjoining streets within 200 yards of another cooperative landmark, St Cuthbert's headquarters at Ponton Street. So many consecutive entries of neighbours in the Register of Shareholders indicates that they bought £1 shares on a basis not unlike present-day crowd sourcing. In another illustration of mutuality, a cluster of six engineers at Hillhousefield, Leith each bought a £1 shareholding and altogether Leithers subscribed 16% of the ECBC capital. With one in six shareholders resident in Leith it was not

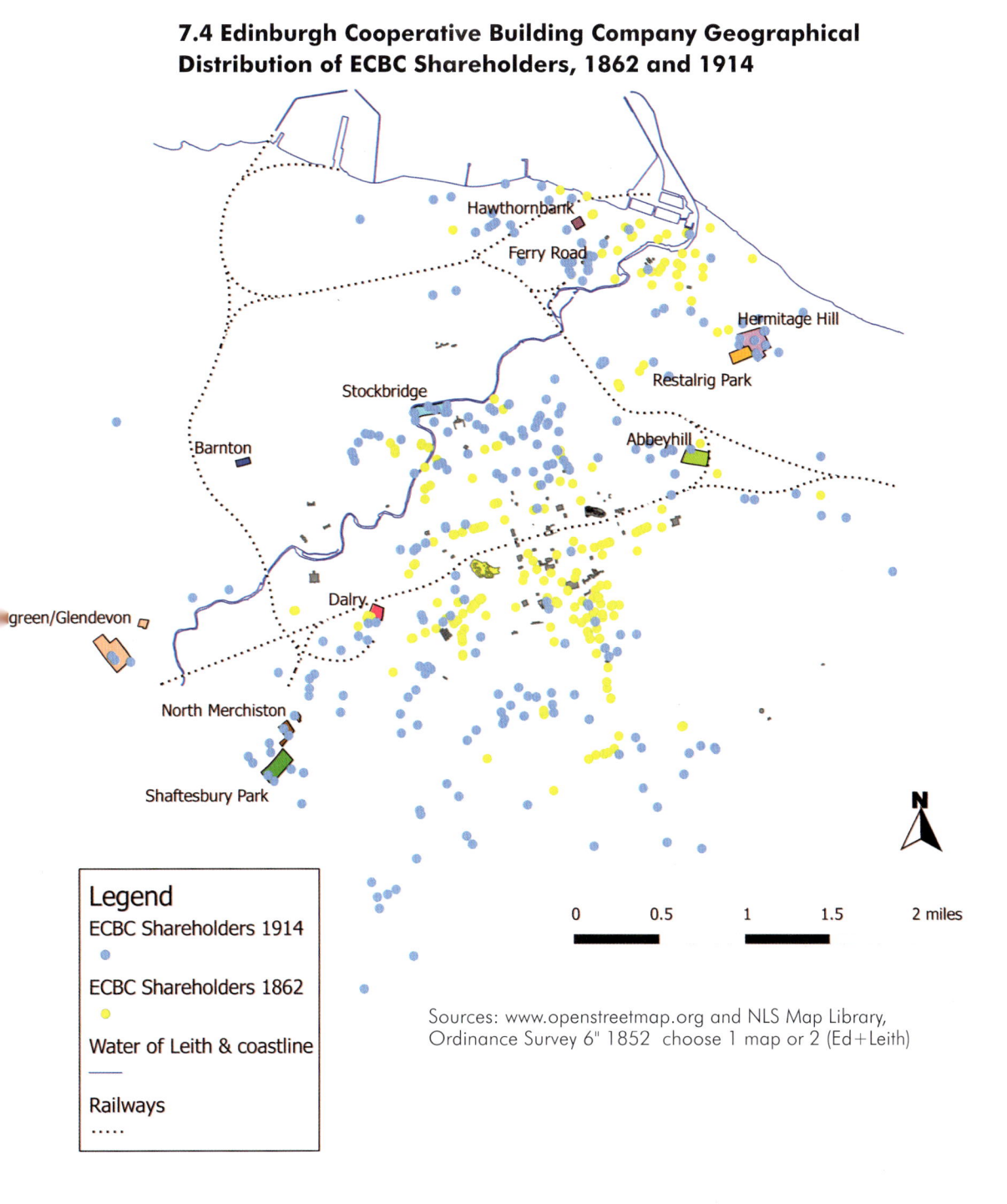

7.4 Edinburgh Cooperative Building Company Geographical Distribution of ECBC Shareholders, 1862 and 1914

Legend
ECBC Shareholders 1914
●
ECBC Shareholders 1862
●
Water of Leith & coastline
—
Railways
·····

Sources: www.openstreetmap.org and NLS Map Library, Ordinance Survey 6" 1852 choose 1 map or 2 (Ed+Leith)

Structural Strength

surprising that so many of the ECBC homes were eventually built there.

'At half-past six o'clock, the foundation-stone... was laid by the Rev. Dr. Begg... There was placed in the cavity of the stone a glass bottle containing a copy of Dr Begg's pamphlet on working men's houses, a portrait of Dr Begg, copies of the Edinburgh newspapers, etc. The stone having been fixed in its place, the Rev. Mr. Muir engaged in prayer.'[8] The *second* ECBC street, Hugh Miller Place, was under construction in April 1863.

Begg's second oration was just as positive as his first. Construction he noted, 'is now in the hands of the working men themselves, and... it is in good hands.'[9] He was 'delighted to see that Edinburgh has taken the lead... which will have (an) effect on the whole of Scotland.' This national perspective was important. Begg used it to motivate and indeed to challenge individuals in positions of authority. For example, he noted the successes amongst 'Our English friends' and drew attention specifically to a 'most successful' recent building association in Birmingham which was 'buying up all land around the city and prosecuting their work most vigorously.' Begg concluded his speech by saying 'Let the workmen of Edinburgh show [Prime Minister] Lord Palmerston these houses and tell him that Scotland is able for the task of curing her own social evils and... that the only way of effectively curing them is by the universal establishment of comfortable homes.' (Cheers).

The issue of the availability of land – and thus its price as an element of building costs – was a perennial cause for concern for the ECBC. Based on natural justice, Begg made the case for improved access to building land:

> 'It is a very monstrous thing that human life and comfort should be sacrificed in Edinburgh on such a large scale by causes so easily removable. If the town were perishing for want of water, and if copious springs and large lakes in the neighbourhood were kept up by the civic authorities and the managers of benevolent institutions, the public and Parliament would soon interfere. The city of Edinburgh is suffering at this moment in the most dreadful way from a similar cause, and the

principles applicable to water ought equally to be applied to the unreasonable and cruel hoarding of land.'

The first parcel of land acquired in 1861 by the Directors of the ECBC was obtained from James Haig, the well-known whisky distillers. The initial site of 1.17 acres site adjoining the Canonmills distillery occupied the western end of Water Lane and was bounded on two sides by the Water of Leith. The unsatisfactory nature of the site was condemned as a nuisance by the Prime Minister, Lord Palmerston:

> 'It not only receives the sewage matter and refuse of probably 100,000 people but is also made the receptacle of all the horrible abominations which leak and ouse out of the diverse glue-works, paper-mills, chemical works, and gas-works. . . and from a gigantic distillery, which discharges enormous quantities of hot and acrid wash into its already polluted channel.' [10]

Since the River Thames in the summer of 1858 produced the 'Great Stink', and caused Parliament to suspend its sittings, Palmerston's comment was rather mean-spirited. Though foul-smelling, the Stockbridge building site was affordable and available, and so the ECBC paid £20 per annum feu duty for the property with opportunities to obtain further lots if business justified it. In its favour, too, though Palmerston did not see it as such, was its proximity to the 'diverse' industries of Canonmills and Silvermills which sustained communities and shops in the Bedford Street area where many locked-out stonemasons and ECBC shareholders lived and worked.

The ECBC engaged its own building tradesmen supervised by the Company's general manager, James Colville (in post 1861-90), and sold the properties to shareholders and the general public at a price judged to yield a fair return on the outlay. The ECBC prospectus conveyed something of the organisational strength and the financial journey upon which it had embarked:

> 'The Edinburgh Cooperative Building Company have commenced a block of houses for working men near

Happy Homes

7.5 Stockbridge colonies 1896 map

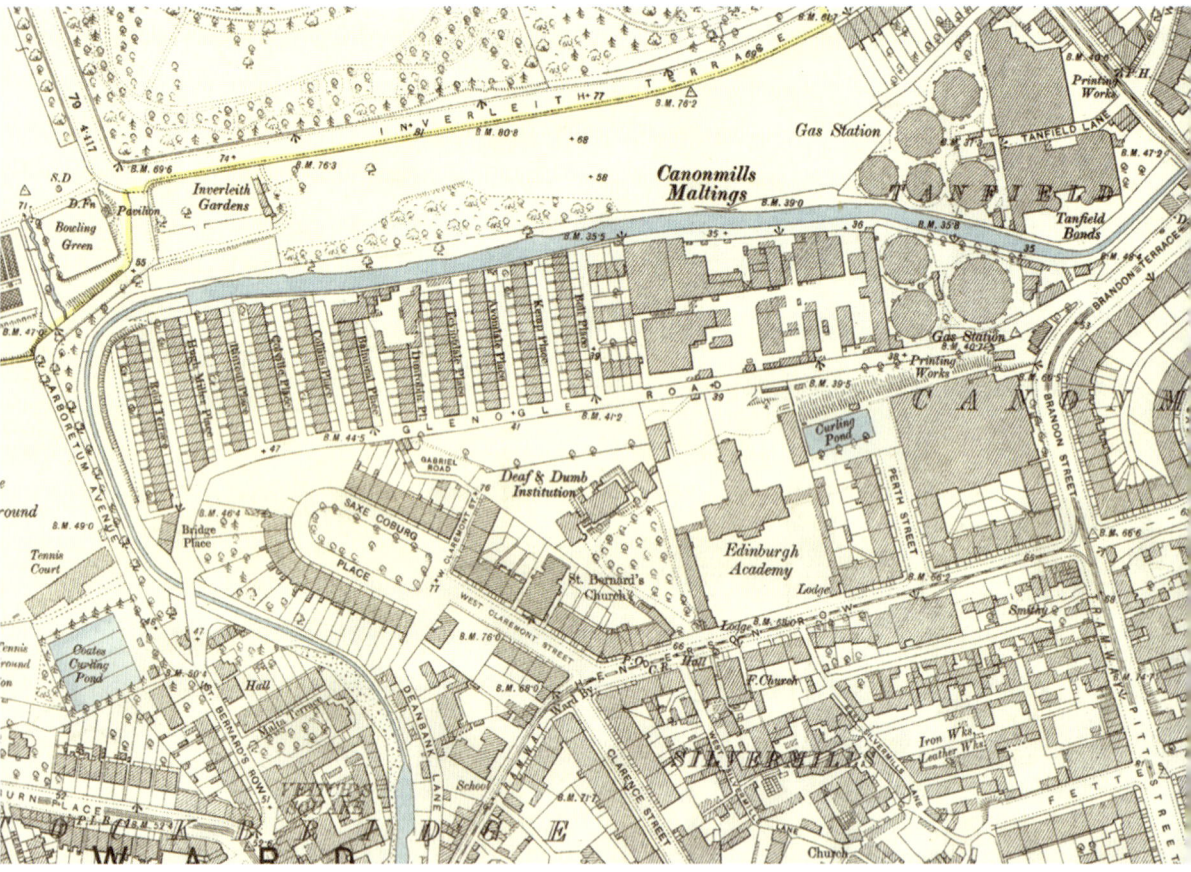

Source: Reproduced with the permission of NLS

Stockbridge, and if they are duly supported, any number of similar houses may soon be erected. The present object is to build and sell the houses, and with the money thus received, not only to pay interest on the capital, but to build and sell again, until the supply of workmen's houses shall meet demand. Everything, however, depends on the energy of the men themselves.'

Structural Strength

7.6 Stockbridge Floor Plan, 'low doors' and 'high doors'

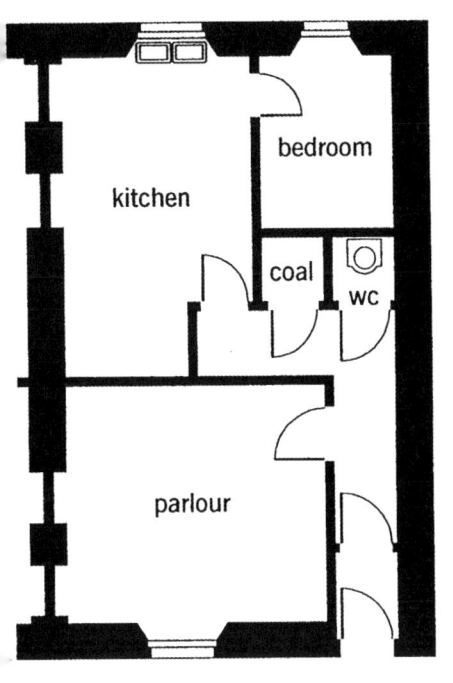

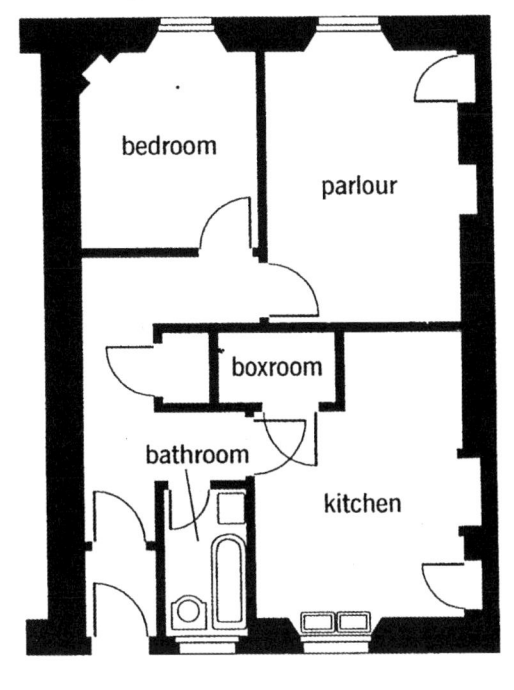

Typical early 'low door' house

Later 'low door' house with bathroom
(e.g. 15 Teviotdale Place, Glenogle Road)

Happy Homes

Joiner	Blacksmith	Carter
Painter	Draughtsman	Plumber
Builder	Mason	Plasterer

8.1 Trades plaques

8. From Strength to Strength

IN ITS FIRST year the ECBC built and sold eight houses in Reid Terrace. By 1863 and the publication of the 2nd Annual Report the directors were 'happy in being able to state that the whole five blocks of 40 houses are now completed, occupied and paid for'.[1] Two further plots of land, also obtained from James Haig, and further terraces (Hugh Miller Place and Rintoul Place) were underway, financed by the profits on the Reid Terrace houses and by further subscriptions of share capital. In the second year of operations 54 houses were completed with some sold as what would now be termed 'off plan' – before building was even begun. This improved the liquidity of the Company. Profits of 12% were recorded in the first six months and by 1863, only eighteen months after commencing building work, the ECBC was able to declare a 10% dividend to shareholders which prompted a surge of interest from new investors.[2]

The scale and speed of ECBC home-building, while impressive, seemed unlikely to satisfy demand and so ECBC feued a further 1.5 acres in October 1862, this time at Elizafield (North Leith), another location where several ECBC shareholders lived. Within months, in fact, on the 15 March 1863, the Rev James Begg and others took part in a third foundation stone ceremony, laid this time by Councillor Henderson of Leith. Two months later, in May 1863, the Company had already roofed half of the planned 44 homes at what became known as Hawthornbank Place and Terrace.[3] These Colony houses with the trademark external staircases sold at 6.5% above the Stockbridge prices, and were described by the ECBC as 'a class much superior to any this company has hitherto built'.[4] This was one reason why 'persistence', that is, continuity of residence, at the Hawthornbank Colonies was one of the highest of all the streets constructed by the ECBC.

8.2 Stockbridge ECBC Glenogle Road plaque

These plaques were installed at Stockbridge, Restalrig, Abbeyhill, Dalry, North Merchiston, Shaftesbury with only the name and development changed

By the 3rd Annual General Meeting in 1864 a total of 132 'Colony' houses had been built and sold and, encouraged by a record profit that year and handsome dividend, there was little difficulty in 1865 to the following year to obtain the remaining £6,600 to bring the share capital to its fully paid-up level of £10,000. A more modest dividend of 7.5% in 1865 was accompanied by the creation of both Contingent and Reserve funds designed to equalise dividend distributions and 'give stability to the Company' so as to offer the 'best guarantee the public can have that (the Company) is managed with prudence'.[5] It was an astute financial tactic.

In addition to tight financial management by the Treasurer (Kemp) three structural factors enhanced the prospects of the ECBC in the 1860s. One was concerned with the conveyancing documents themselves. These stipulated that the ECBC houses were to be:

> '. . . substantially built with stone and lime and roofed with slate and, exclusive of chimney tops, not to exceed forty-six feet. . . it shall be unlawful to convert or permit to be converted any of the dwelling houses. . . into shebeens or brothels. . . or to have any cow house, pig house or manufactory.'
> Source: NRS, RS27/2354, feu disposition 11 Sept 1861

Added to these quality controls regarding materials and labour, the clauses governing permissible activities ensured certain types of tenants and owners could be excluded, and a degree of social control applied to manage the tone of the Colony developments.

The second factor concerned the design of the ECBC properties themselves. This owed a debt to the model dwellings at Pilrig and the features of Rosebank Cottages. The ECBC floor plans (Fig. 7.6) preserved home life on a single level – one family occupied the ground floor level and another the floor above which was accessed by a distinctive stone staircase with a wrought iron balustrade. In contrast to the undifferentiated space of one- and two-room tenement flats, the intention was to define room functions and uses more clearly in ECBC houses. Unlike back-to-back English terraces, the design incorporated through ventilation to both ground and first floor levels and economised on building

8.3 Hawthornbank 1864 (Elizafield) and Ferry Road site

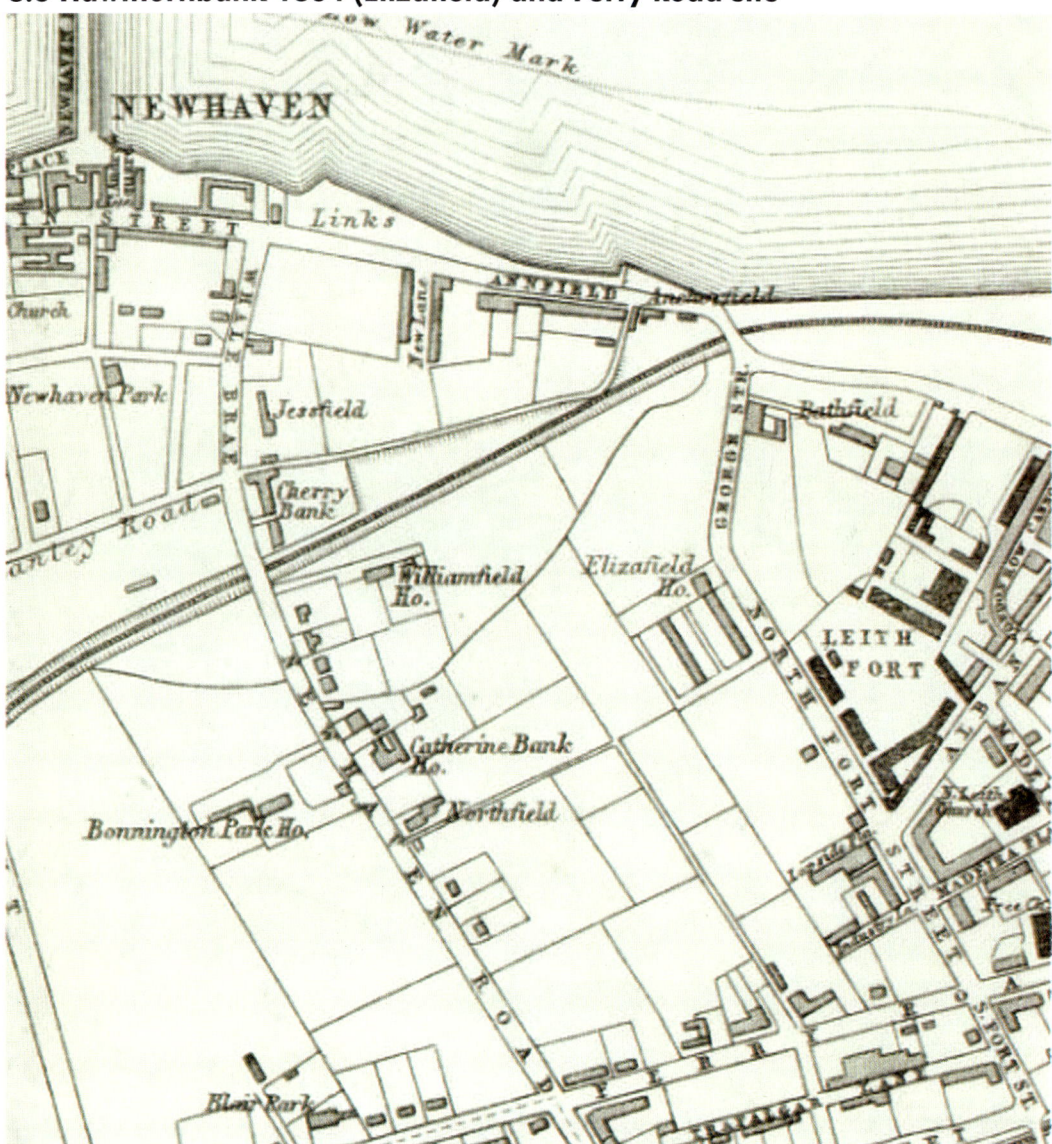

Source: Plan of Edinburgh and Leith with suburbs. John Bartholomew for Post Office Directory (1864) with permission of NLS

Note: Elizatield House is shown adjoining two parallel streets – Hawthornbank Place and Terrace. The vacant rectangle below 'ERR' in Ferry Road is the Henderson Place site. The eastern end of the rectangle is Trafalgar Street.

Happy Homes

8.4 Hawthornbank Terrace

PHOTO: John Reiach

8.5 Hawthornbank corner sign
Typical ECBC chiselled stone street name

costs through shared foundations and roofs along the entire length of a terrace. The external rather than an internal staircase itself was estimated to pare £42 from the selling price of a house – a saving estimated to be at least 25% on the final building costs. Taken together, these design features were highly original and introduced a different vision of urban living for working families in Edinburgh. External stairs were themselves unoriginal; they were, and still are, visible in fishing and agricultural settlements throughout Scotland. But what was novel about the ECBC design was that the staircase ran at right angles to the house, not parallel to it, and did so in a densely packed urban setting. Internal space was not squandered on a hall or corridor, and the overall estate plan economised on street widths and so increased the extent of building land. The distinctive result enabled each household to have a self-contained dwelling with a separate entrance, small private garden, and drying area, as well as a water supply, range, sink, and W.C.

The third factor was to develop a financial package to address the question: how could workmen afford to own their house? The answer was to develop a mortgage plan for would-be homeowners. In a somewhat off-hand tone, James Begg suggested that saving on 'snuffing and smoking' would be sufficient to fund a mortgage! More seriously, though, he explained how the ECBC made it possible to own a ground floor 'Colony' house in Stockbridge with two rooms and a kitchen costing £130:

> 'Any man who has £5 now can get a house of his own because the Property Investment Companies (such as the ECBC) will advance the balance of £125. If you were to rent such a house it would cost £11 per annum. The Edinburgh Cooperative Building Company charges £13 per annum – that is £2 per annum more, but only for fourteen years. If a man were a snuffer and a smoker. . . he will save all the difference between the rent and the purchase-money upon his tobacco, if he choose to deny himself.'
>
> Source: J. Begg, 'Report of the Committee on Houses for the Working Classes in connection with Social Morality' submitted to the General Assembly of the Free Church of Scotland, May 1862

8.6 Clothes poles, like this one in Dalry, and barley twist railings were a distinctive and standard feature all the early ECBC Colony developments

The average annual rental of over 23,000 *tenanted* properties in Edinburgh in 1861 was £16.67.[6] So Begg's illustration based on a rent of £11 p.a. might just seem achievable as a general approach to creating affordable happy homes. However, in Edinburgh the average annual rental paid by 1750 tenants employed in the building trades was £6.60 p.a. – just 60% of the £11 on which Begg's calculation was based. So the owner of an ECBC Colony house required a predictable income such as a widows' pension or annuity, or the steady employment of skilled workers, or a degree of job security as in the case of grocers and bakers, merchants and makers. Only they could afford an annual rental in the £11-13 p.a. range required to be ECBC owners. Of course, family members might contribute to the household budget, lodgers provided a lifeline for some families, and a percentage of workers in each trade earned above the average wage. Even so, for many workers in the building trades £11 was beyond their financial comfort zone. To encourage ownership, Begg also appealed to family values and legacies by explaining that in 'fourteen years. . . the house will be your own, and will belong to your children after you'. It was not just an emotional appeal. It was hard-nosed realism regarding household budgets. After fourteen years workers would own their home; they would never have to pay rent again!

The standardised rental index shows how individual occupations compare with the city-wide average. Masons paid rent of £6.15 on average, equivalent to 50.3% of the city-wide average rent. Rev. Dr James Begg occupied Newington Free Church Manse, rental value £75 p.a.

The occasion for Begg's 'Snuff and Smoking' speech was the ceremony to lay the Foundation Stone[7] for the second row of Stockbridge 'Colony' houses – Hugh Miller Place – just eighteen months after the start of building at Reid Terrace where all forty houses had been sold. The great problem of house accommodation for the working classes', Begg stated, was 'a most important social question for Scotland'. He also criticised Edinburgh town councillors as the governors of Heriot's Hospital for hoarding 33 acres of undeveloped land between Leith Walk and Broughton, and heaped scorn on them for their reluctance to relocate the Cattle Market and other land intensive activities

Table 8.1 An Edinburgh Hierarchy: Tenants Rents by Selected Occupations 1861				
tenant's occupation	number of rentals	average rent (£ p.a.)	standard deviation (£)	standardised rental index
carter	207	4.40	2.15	36.0
smith	247	5.61	3.29	45.9
mason	427	6.15	3.98	50.3
slater	72	6.16	5.03	50.4
plasterer	86	6.63	5.21	54.3
painter	318	6.84	6.56	56.0
joiner	453	6.96	4.13	57.0
wright	117	7.44	5.34	60.9
cabinetmaker	334	7.80	5.92	63.8
plumber	83	8.96	7.61	73.3
teacher	102	34.46	44.57	282.0
bank clerk	21	35.85	19.56	293.4
ALL CATEGORIES	**23,032**	**12.22**	**19.05**	**100.0**

'to some locality a mile out of town.'[8] 'Happy Homes' for working people depended on a highly sensitive issue – a sufficient supply of building land – and this remained the core problem for the ECBC for fifty years.

The Stockbridge and Hawthornbank houses sold quickly. This established a robust financial position for the Company. But it also meant another building site was required – urgently. If not, then the momentum and public confidence in the ECBC itself might be compromised. Worse still, perhaps, the skilled workforce assembled by the ECBC would drift away if there was no work and so the entire cooperative enterprise might falter and fail. When a few hundred yards from Hawthornbank another site became available the ECBC acquired it. Like their previous sites, this too was on the margins of the built-up area in 1864. But unlike the previous sites, the 1.75 acre plot was on the corner of a major thoroughfare (Ferry Road see Fig. 8.7) and the sixty Trafalgar Street and Henderson Place tenement homes that were built were 30-35% more expensive than self-contained ECBC branded Stockbridge and Hawthornbank Colony housing.[9] To make sales even more difficult, the official re-naming of the street as Ferry Road – and meaningless numbers 147-85 – confused would-be buyers as to their exact location.[10] These were was costly decisions. Three years after the latest

Source: NRS, Valuation Rolls VR100/33-37; R. Rodger, 'Property and inequality: housing dynamics in a nineteenth-century city', *Economic History Review* 75:3, 2002 (Open Access at https://doi.org/10.1111/ehr.13138)

Happy Homes

PHOTO: John Reiach

8.7 ECBC Ferry Road and Trafalgar Street tenements
(see bottom right hand corner of Map 8.4)

foundation stone was laid, the ECBC manager, James Colville was still placing newspaper adverts in the Leith Burghs newspaper, *The Pilot*, and attending the 'Show Homes' in person in attempt to interest potential buyers in the flats. Capital was tied up for some years and obliged the Building Company to become a landlord. It took structural strength within the ECBC to address and overcome such a setback.

The ECBC's business model was dependent on the overlapping development of building sites, with house sales on one site used to refinance the next. In 1865, and over the next three years, the ECBC undertook extended discussions with Heriot's Trustees to build houses on their Ferniehill estate, a very extensive triangle of land known as Leith Walk Nurseries. Bounded by the modern East London Street, McDonald Road and Bellevue Road, the Nurseries were about twice the area now occupied by Lothian Buses central garage at Annandale Street. The ECBC received 'a cold reception' from Heriot's Trustees not only over this site, which remained substantially undeveloped for the next forty years, but more generally according to the *Courant's* account of land hoarding:

> 'The Heriot's Hospital property in the vicinity of Leith ought not to be allowed to lie over any longer in its present unproductive state, as it is now manifest that along the whole line of this the future principal thoroughfare of the city [Leith Walk], the ground would be all taken up for feuing within a year or two, were it offered to the public on moderate terms.'[11]

Failure to strike a deal was largely down to price. For the first phase of the Stockbridge development in 1861 land was available at £18 per acre feu duty but three years later had risen 67% to £30. In 1864 the shareholders were informed that the company had entered negotiations in Leith for building land priced at £25 per acre feu duty – £2 below the price set on other Leith plots in which the Directors had expressed an interest. The impact of rising land prices was of genuine concern in the mid- and late-1860s since, first, this reduced the profit margin and thus the dividend to shareholders; and secondly, because of the 'difficulty of obtaining ground in or very near the city (which) had forced the society to build their houses in a less advantageous situation.'[12] Ferry Road was a salutary episode.

During 1866 and 1867 the ECBC was involved, often simultaneously, in negotiations regarding twelve sites – at Ferniehill; Brougham Street; Gladstone Terrace; Morrison Street; Maryfield (Abbeyhill) owned by Lady Menzies; Haymarket in lieu of the Morrison Street site when James Walker's trustees welched on that deal; four acres at Bonnington owned by James Steel; ground owned by Trinity Hospital in Leith, and other plots in Leith at Pitt, George and North Fort Streets; and a five acre site at Restalrig Park. No doubt there were other sites that were considered and rejected as unsuitable even before negotiations got underway.

A shrewd business practice concerning the acquisition of building sites was used by the ECBC. An initial parcel of land was feued to test the viability of the area. If there was interest and the houses sold quickly adjacent portions were promptly acquired from the landowner. This happened with two extensions at Stockbridge, the last of which was for five acres in 1867. Anxiety regarding future building stances was lessened when two of the twelve sites under consideration resulted in deals with the landowners Lady Menzies (Maryfield, Abbeyhill 1866) and James

8.8 Abbeyhill Colonies (Maryfield or Norton Park)

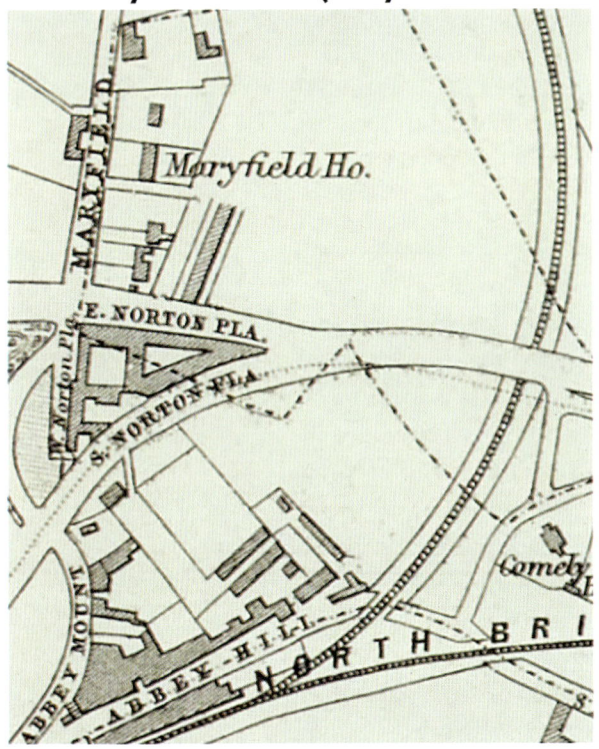

Source: Plan of Edinburgh and Leith with suburbs. John Bartholomew for Post Office Directory (1876 and 1876) reproduced with permission of NLS

Walker's Trustees (Dalry, 1867). At the 6th Annual General Meeting shareholders were informed that the 'Directors were fortunate to secure by way of trial, one acre of land, on which the first foundation was laid only in November last' (Maryfield 1866) and 'seeing the demand for houses in this new quarter the Directors have feued two more acres which they hope to cover with houses in the course of this and the following year.' Hemmed in by the Edinburgh, North Leith and Granton Railway, a further six acres were obtained in 1868 because, as the 7th Annual Report stated, 'The proximity of this ground to the densely populated districts of the Canongate and south east side of the town will greatly facilitate the sale of the houses'.[13]

The break-up of the Walker estate of Easter and Wester Dalry was a response to the development of Edinburgh's railway version of 'spaghetti' junction. The development of the Caledonian Railway route (now the Western Approach Road) and the Glasgow and Edinburgh Railway expansion around Haymarket station and the goods yards nearby compromised the western extension of the New Town. Ever alert, the ECBC Directors recognised the opportunity for housing development at Dalry and 'secured three acres of ground in this daily improving part of the city. . . with every prospect of success as inquiries after houses. . . are daily being made'.[14] Only a year later and with 32 houses sold, the shareholders read that:

> 'This feu has fully borne out the expectations of the Directors and from its eligibility and fine situation, there is little fear but

8.9 Abbeyhill Colonies, Waverley Place

that the whole of the houses erected will find ready purchasers.'[15]

A few years later, in 1877, St Cuthbert's Cooperative opened their second branch at 31 Caledonian Terrace just a few yards from the ECBC Dalry Colony houses and embedded in the dense tenements of James Steel's Caledonian feu, also obtained from James Walker's trustees.

Restalrig Park, Lochend Road in South Leith was the third ECBC new area of land acquired in the financial year 1867-68. The 7th Annual General Meeting of shareholders were informed of a 10% dividend distribution and, significantly, of the purchase of 'five acres of most eligible ground'. The purchase was financed partly by the sale of previously rented properties in Leith. The Directors exuded positivity about Restalrig:

> 'It is within ten minutes walk of the centre of Leith, commands an extensive view of Edinburgh and the Forth, and surrounding country, and is so well adapted to the

Happy Homes

8.10 Dalry

Argyll Terrace, Dalry, looking west

8.11 Restalrig colonies, Lochend Road

PHOTO: John Reiach

requirements of that fast increasing burgh that the directors have commenced operations by laying the foundations of thirty-two houses.'[16]

The strength of the Stockbridge, Dalry and Abbeyhill Colonies, as acknowledged by the ECBC itself in its Annual Reports, was the 'proximity' of its housing developments to concentrations of employment – artisans, clerks, and shopkeepers – for whom the rents of ECBC houses were affordable. The Directors' explanation for the sluggish interest in Restalrig properties was that the new properties were hidden from view by 'a row of old houses entirely closing up the front'.[17] This is not an entirely convincing explanation. More likely is the fact that Leith rents were generally lower than those in comparable Edinburgh tenements and, therefore, the Restalrig Colonies were considered too expensive by some and unaffordable by other Leith workers. Given the presence of Leith-based masons in the ECBC it is perhaps surprising that the Leith Colony developments – Ferry Road and

Restalrig – presented problems of one kind or another for the ECBC. Or perhaps the hesitancy at Restalrig was just an intimation simply of a sense of general economic recession in 1870 which also affected the building industry. As the Annual Report in 1871 noted:

> 'The past year has not been so successful as previous years owing to the great flatness that has existed in all branches of trade, and the change that has taken place in the building trade.'[18]

In 1871 the ECBC undertook what in modern terms would be called a ten-year review. The early years of the ECBC recalled the enthusiasm for the cooperative mission and a positive and rapid uptake of workers' housing. The language of the late-1860s certainly reflected that. '(T)he operations of the Company continue as prosperous as hitherto' (Stockbridge); 'demand here also has been greater than we could meet (Maryfield); 'the success of last year has been continued' and 'this feu has fully borne out the expectation of the Directors' (Dalry). And overall, there was 'a steady increase of sales in every year since the Company commenced operations'.[19]

In its first ten years homes for over 4,200 people had been built. The average cost was £171, and 96% of the 872 built by the ECBC had been sold.[20] The ECBC employed 250 workmen and had feued and developed 30 acres of ground.[21] It was one of the largest building firms in the city and in a single decade the ECBC had contributed 2% to the housing stock of Edinburgh and almost 15% of new housebuilding in the city during the years 1861-71. A dividend of 12.5% in 1870 was considered indicative of the 'undoubted stability' of the Company after trading for ten years trading.

It was deemed a highly satisfactory record and the existence of the ECBC was 'extended indefinitely'. With this open time horizon, the Directors could introduce 'a scheme for the sale of houses by instalments' which together with 'the twin scheme for receiving money on deposit, gave a new lease of life to the company', though the 'only real impediment to a lengthened existence in the future seemed to have been the increasing difficulty of obtaining land in any quantity near the industries of the city'.

Table 8.2 Houses Built by the Edinburgh Cooperative Building Company 1862-72

street	number built	cost (£)	average price(£)	street	number built	cost (£)	average price(£)
(1) Stockbridge				**(3) Abbeyhill**			
Reid Terr	40	4992	125	Maryfield	47	7623	156
Hugh Miller Place	33	4784	145	Alva Place	47	7796	162
Rintoul Place	32	4866	152	Lady Menzies Pl.	46	8021	174
Colville Place	30	5123	171	Regent Place	51	8172	160
Collins Place	30	4532	151	Waverley Place	47	8038	171
Bell Place	32	4830	151	Carlyle Place	47	8438	180
Kemp Place	30	4940	165	**(4) Dalry**			
Glenogle Place	8	1330	166	Cobden Terr	16	2655	166
Glenogle Terr	8	1220	153	Bright Terr	16	2655	166
Avondale Place	30	5125	171	McLaren Terr	10	1670	167
Teviotdale Place	16	3295	206	Douglas Terr	16	2655	166
Balmoral Place	24	2664	128	Argyll Terr	16	2655	166
Dunrobin Place	8	1440	180	Atholl Terr	16	2655	166
				Breadalbane Terr	16	2655	166
				Breadalbane Cott	2	420	210
(2) Leith				Lewis Terr	16	3170	198
Hawthornbank Place	22	3577	163	Walker Terr	16	3780	236
Hawthornbank Terr	22	3577	163	**(5) Restalrig**			
Henderson Place	43	10155	236	Woodville Terr	16	3140	196
Trafalgar Street	17	4040	238	Woodbine Terr	32	5273	165
				Thornville Terr	16	2495	156

Source: Based on J. Begg, *Happy Homes for Working Men* (Edinburgh 1872 edn.) Appendix III.

Table 8.3 Share Transfers May 1867-May 1869

	building trades	other trades	clerks merchants	ladies & no stated work	companies
sold	445	490	37	135	173
purchased	156	459	220	282	163

Source: NRS GD1/772, Report by the Finance Committee 27 Sept. 1869

Yet there was real cause for concern. Firstly, the Finance Committee reported a pattern of share transfers in the late-1860s which showed a structural shift in the ownership of the ECBC (Table 8.3). Workers in the building trades had moved decisively away from share-owning and thus from a direct interest in the governance of the cooperative. It was not other trades, however, that had adopted the cooperative gospel; it was clerks and dealers, shopkeepers and merchants, who with women and a class of 'rentiers' obtained their income from dividends, rents and profits.

Secondly, ownership of ECBC shares was one thing; ownership of Colony properties was another. Individuals increasingly acquired multiple properties, as for example, in Hugh Miller Place where by 1910 numbers 1-12, 21-24, and 26-32 were all in the hands of Miss C. D. Hamilton and her family.[22] In one sense, the ECBC had itself become an instrument of capital accumulation for a rentier or landlord class.

Thirdly, a copy-cat firm, the Industrial Cooperative Building Company, was formed by stonemasons in 1868. By its very name and with a building site next to that of the ECBC one at Restalrig Park, the ICBC built houses which were indistinguishable at first sight to those of the ECBC.[23] Industrial Road was the spine from which several streets of 'Colony style' houses were started in 1868. The firm's timing was poor, however, as the ECBC itself discovered with several successive 'flat' years in succession from 1869. The ICBC was under-capitalised – equivalent to only 7% of the subscribed ECBC capital – and this was critical since, unlike the ECBC, it had been unable to offload its completed properties and experienced serious cash-flow problems. There was no cushion or Reserve Fund, and the ICBC went into voluntary liquidation in 1875. Undeterred, however, the company was taken over by two of the ICBC partners, Kinross-born stonemasons William and Alexander Fingzies. They built 215 houses in Summerfield, Lindean (previously

8.12 Copycat Development

Industrial Road, Fingzies Place – built by Industrial Co-operative Building Company with entry from front and rear to upper and lower flats

Waverley) Place, Noble, Parkvale, Rosevale, Fingzies, Elm, Cochrane, and Somerset Places, and the northern section of Restalrig Road before it, too, went out of business. With net liabilities of £4,577, and realised assets of £182, only £67 or 1.5% was paid to secured debtors. Unsecured debtors (£2,205) received nothing.[24]

A fourth cause for ECBC concern, as reflected in rising land prices in the 1860s, was the greatly increased competition for residential sites. The feuing system fuelled this process and contributed to the boom and bust familiar to housebuilders everywhere but there was another structural factor affecting the market for land in the 1860s.[25] This was the emergence of highly localised building associations. In the Lauriston area (near Tollcross) for example, the Glen Street Building Association was only one of eight such associations – Lauriston, Lauriston Gardens, Lauriston Place, Lauriston Park, North Lauriston Gardens, West Lauriston Place, and South Lauriston Building Associations. A small group of individuals formed an Association of would-be neighbours and paid an advance to a builder and gave an undertaking to purchase a flat on completion of the building. This commitment enabled the builder to raise the balance of the necessary working capital. In the case of the 225 household heads in the eight Building Associations in the Lauriston area, the deposits came from a mostly professional and commercial class, though the largest single group (30%) of investors were women, mostly living on income from bonds and rents.[26] Across the Meadows a similar development existed – the Hope Park, Bower, Meadow, Meadow Park, United, Livingstone, Melville, and Sciennes Building Associations. Over eighty such Building Associations were active in Edinburgh in the years 1869-74 (Table 8.4). In effect, by pooling their commitment to purchase flats and providing a limited amount of start-up capital to the builder, these associations were equivalent to terminating building societies and, as the highly specific names indicate, they were often concerned only with a single or perhaps a few tenements in a specific street. There were over eighty such Building Associations active in Edinburgh in the years 1869-74.

Whereas a Building Association was a closed group in which members were beneficiaries of a specific housing project, with Building *Societies* investors' deposits were made available to builders and developers in return for a dividend or loan repayment on the completion of a tenement project. Investors expected a return to the capital invested; they did not expect to move into a property themselves. These were in effect Investment Societies and their names reflected not the name of a street or district but a more generic investment function: the Amicable Property Investment Building Society; Edinburgh Mutual Investment Building Society; Fourth Provincial Property Investment and Building Society; and Permanent Scottish Union Property Investment Society. Indeed, the Edinburgh property market also attracted funds from investors and building societies outwith the city, such as the Kirkcaldy Property Investment Society and the Musselburgh Building and Investment Society.[27]

While the scale of individual Building Associations and Societies was generally modest, their investors were in competition with the ECBC. As a result, the ECBC entered a new phase with some anxiety with the manager, James Colville, and his fellow Directors incapable of securing a site on the south of the city.

Table 8.4 Building Associations in Edinburgh 1869-74

Abbotsford	Glengyle	Meadowside	South Grindlay Street
Albert	Grange Provident	Melville	South Lauriston
Albert Place	Grindlay Street	Midlothian	Spittalfield
Argyle	Grove	Montague Street	Springfield
Bainfield	Hope Park	Montgomery	Stewartfield
Barcaple	Ivanhoe	Montgomery Place	Teviot
Bower	Kenilworth	Newington	Thistle
Brougham Place	Lauriston	North Lauriston Gdns	Trafalgar
Bruntsfield	Lauriston Gardens	North Meadowside	Tynecastle
Burgess	Lauriston Park	Oxford Street	Tynecastle 2nd
Burns	Lauriston Place	Panmure Place	Union
Caledonian	Leamington	Richmond	Valleyfield
Caledonian Place	Leven Lodge	Rob Roy	Victorian
Dalry	Leven Terrace	Rockville	Viewforth
Douglas	Livingstone	Rose	Waverley
Drumdryan Street	Lord Clyde	Rosehall Place	West Claremont Street
East London Street	Lorne	St. Leonard's	West Lauriston Place
Forrest Road	Lutton Place	St. Margaret's	West Meadow Place
Gardner	Mayfield	Saxe Coburg	Windsor
Gillespie Crescent	Meadow	Sciennes	Working Men's Provident
Glen Street	Meadow Park	Southern	

Source: NRS, Register of Sasines, Abridgements and Index of Names 1869-74.

Happy Homes

Gardens and productive leisure time were part of the ECBC ethos

PHOTO: John Reiach

9. Building Phases

BUILDING the Stockbridge Colonies provided a fifteen-year backbone to the ECBC's activities. 'Three good sized villages of self-contained houses' and two similar villages in Leith 'provided homes for 6,000 people during the 15 years 1861-1876.'[1] The style of housing defined the Colonies in the minds of Edinburgh folk, past and present. Rather than undertake construction on building sites in sequence, the ECBC management developed a synchronous approach by building 'Happy Homes' on two or three sites at the same time. The Leith 'Colonies' of Hawthornbank and the Ferry Road tenement flats provided complementary initiatives to the more extensive Stockbridge site. The possibility of unsold or untenanted homes, or of the oversupply of accommodation in a particular locality, were risks that the ECBC management sought to minimise. Diversification was crucial. The ECBC was also pragmatic about mixing house sales to private individuals and to landlords for rentals. And, by developing mortgage terms suited to and affordable by skilled workers and shopkeepers, these regular repayments steadied cash flow in the ECBC and helped the Company avoid the boom and bust which saw so many builders forced into bankruptcy. The ECBC management also adjusted supply to the specific circumstances of each area, accelerating Dalry to a brisk completion, delaying Restalrig when rental potential and house purchase was sluggish, and successively expanding the Abbeyhill site and, when necessary, building tenements on it at Earlston and Salmond Places.

The ECBC was never independent of market forces. The Company adapted to conditions by phased activity on building sites in different locations, by a mix of trademark terraces and a limited number of tenements, and by developing its deposit and loan arrangements. The ECBC built 'Happy Homes' but sold them on either as a lump sum purchase, or through instalment arrangement (mortgages), or to be rented. Sales released working capital for the next project. By these means the ECBC deployed business strategies to mix and manage risk in the notoriously volatile housebuilding industry.[2]

9.1 Building Phases: Edinburgh Cooperative Building Company 1861-1910

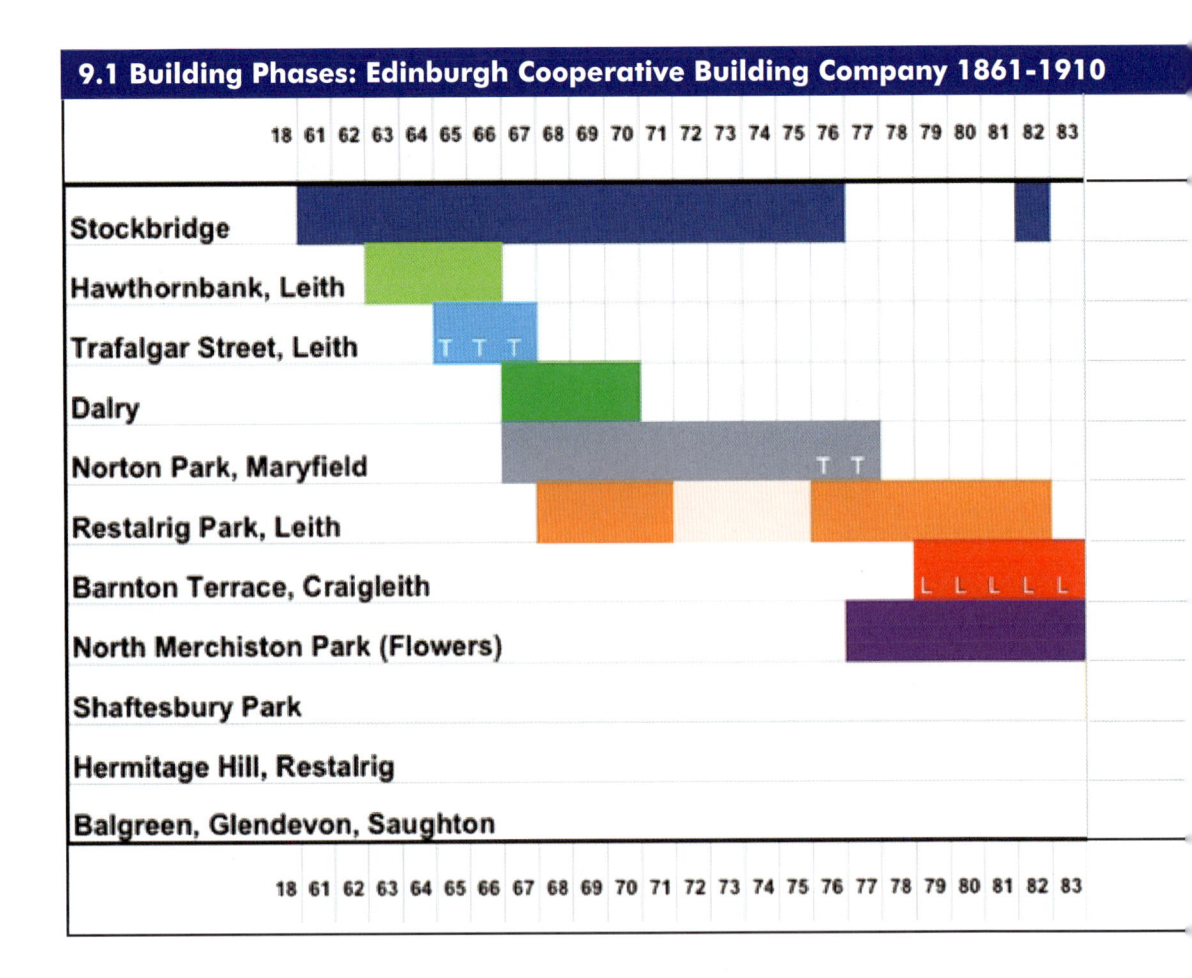

Site	1861-1883
Stockbridge	
Hawthornbank, Leith	
Trafalgar Street, Leith	
Dalry	
Norton Park, Maryfield	
Restalrig Park, Leith	
Barnton Terrace, Craigleith	
North Merchiston Park (Flowers)	
Shaftesbury Park	
Hermitage Hill, Restalrig	
Balgreen, Glendevon, Saughton	

However, these were strategies not without a cost. To maintain shareholder and public confidence the Directors raided the Contingency and Reserve Funds to issue a 7.5% dividend during the tough years of 1872-75 and 1892-93. Otherwise, it was normally 10% or 12.5% and, in 1877, even reached an unprecedented 25% dividend to boost subscriber confidence. The Directors also decided that there was little point in further land purchases on which feu duties were immediately payable when building activity was all but suspended on existing sites. The absence of a plan to acquire land for an eventual upturn in the market was sufficient to cause one shareholder to ponder whether this was an existential moment for the ECBC – 'What should we do?' And then to outline the options: wind up, carry on, or distribute assets.[3]

Yet the consequence of such actions was that when the upturn in the building trade did take place, the ECBC was unable to respond

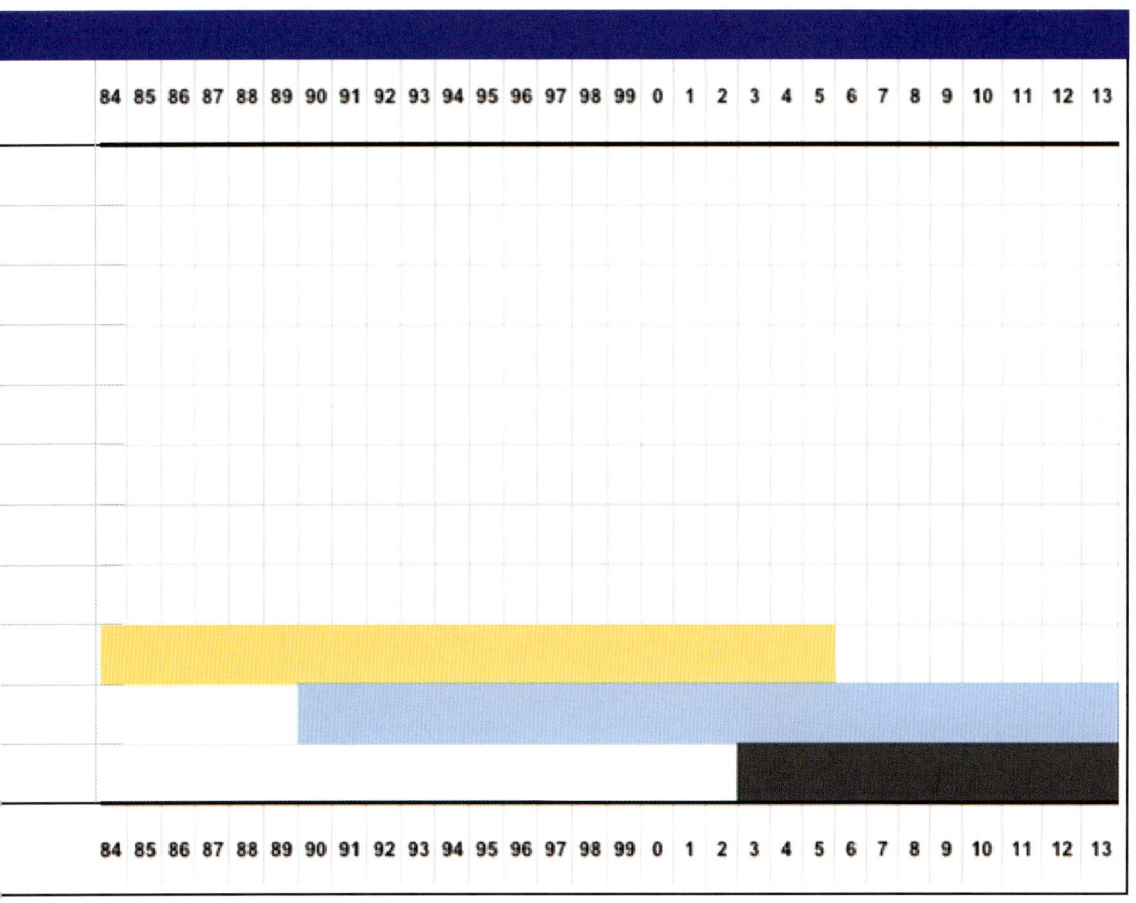

| 84 | 85 | 86 | 87 | 88 | 89 | 90 | 91 | 92 | 93 | 94 | 95 | 96 | 97 | 98 | 99 | 0 | 1 | 2 | 3 | 4 | 5 | 6 | 7 | 8 | 9 | 10 | 11 | 12 | 13 |

promptly. In May 1877, shareholders present at the AGM heard of the 'unprecedented circumstances. . . of having every available house sold.'[4] They had to reconcile this good news, as far as dividends were concerned, with the bad news that there would be some lean years in the future as the ECBC would be almost re-booting the business. As the chairman stated: 'a recommencement of operations' would be necessary.' A decade had passed since the ECBC had last acquired land and still in 1877 the chairman could report no new acquisitions of building sites to the AGM. With land values rising and 'growing more valuable every day', the availability of suitable sites at prices affordable by working men was a genuine threat to the continuation of the ECBC – or as the 15th Annual Report concluded: 'the only real impediment to a lengthened existence. . . seems to be the increasing difficulty of obtaining land in any quantity near the centres of the industries of the city.'[5]

Source: NRS, GD327/488-9; GD1/777/2.
T= tenements, includes Henderson Place; L=letting initially. Restalrig Park 1872-75 no new houses completed

9.2 West Barnton Terrace

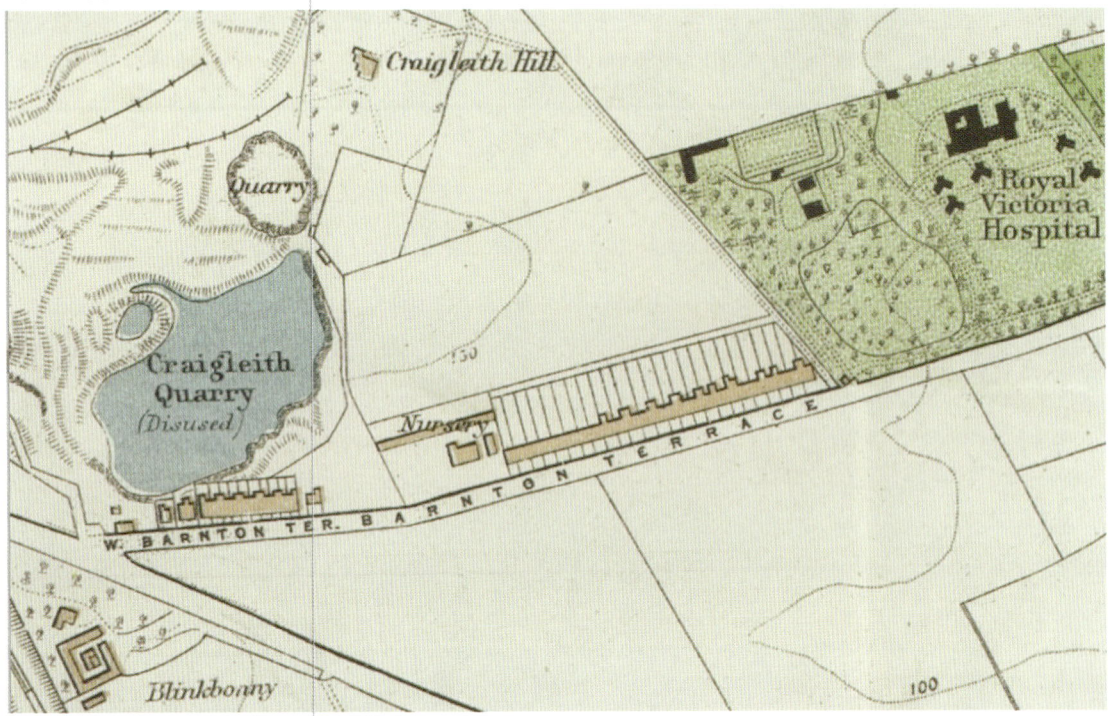

Source: W. & K. Johnston 1910. Reproduced with the permission of NLS

With serious challenges confronting the Company, two contrasting developments in the course of 1877 provided a lifeline for the ECBC. One was at West Barnton Terrace, Craigleith; the other was at Gorgie Mains, North Merchiston. The Craigleith lifeline came about through the Company's manager, James Colville, who was one of the trustees of Robert McNaughton, builder. Colville knew that at the time of his death McNaughton had not fully developed the 3.54 acre site feued from Sir Alexander Maitland in 1871 and successfully encouraged the ECBC to bid for the undeveloped portion.[6] Because the feu charter set out by Maitland applied to the entire site feu-duties had to be divided equally amongst the plots. Consequently, the ECBC was obliged to conform to the standards of the substantial properties already built by McNaughton.[7]

At the Quarterly Meeting of the ECBC in November 1877 it was announced that four 5-bedroom houses were planned, with others to follow. Costing £600, or almost three times the most expensive ECBC homes elsewhere, these Barnton Terrace properties were affordable only by the managers and merchants, employees of insurance and banking firms and others of 'a superior class' – men such as Archibald Blair, a superintendent of various branches of the North British and Mercantile Insurance Company, and Alexander Ross, a New Town grocer and wine merchant. Their social and financial status enabled them to side-step the ECBC's mortgage schemes and to obtain loans independently from the Scottish Property Investment Company and the Fifth Provident Property Investment Company. That the ECBC received a 'good many enquiries' for Barnton Terrace properties from potential house purchasers indicated how much the Edinburgh middle classes valued the swift connection to the city centre anticipated with the impending opening of Blackhall station on the Caledonian Railway's line to Leith.[8] As for the ECBC, Barnton Terrace was a stop-gap strategy. It was not a sustainable solution to the shortfall in supplies of building land suited to working class budgets.

The second lifeline in 1877 stemmed from the acquisition of a five-acre site at Gorgie Mains, North Merchiston, following protracted negotiations with the Merchant Company. Though there was a modest resumption of building activity at Restalrig - Beechwood (1877) and Elmwood Terraces (1878) – it was the North Merchiston Colonies that rekindled the ECBC's construction activities. Like Dalry and Abbeyhill, North Merchiston terraces were shoe-horned into a tricky triangular wedge bounded by railway lines. As with earlier ECBC sites, there was a staged sequence of construction to the 'Flowers' Colonies, or 'Floors', as they were affectionately known, starting with Primrose (1878-79); Myrtle (1878-81); Ivy (1879-83); Laurel (1881); Violet (1881); Daisy (1882-83); Lily (1882-83).

North Merchiston was a genuine 'Colony' – it was outside the municipal boundary and there was no other residential accommodation nearby when construction commenced. Nonetheless it was convenient for the rapidly developing industrial zone which owed much initially to the relocation to Slateford Road of the Caledonian Brewery in 1869 and the establishment of several sizeable employers nearby. These included foundries, bakeries, and engineering companies such as the New Grange Meter Works, St Andrew's Biscuit Co., Grove Biscuit Factory, Edinburgh Iron Foundry, and two laundries. They were part of a general south-westward

Happy Homes

9.3 North Merchiston (Flowers) and Shaftesbury Park Colonies

Source: NLS

Arrows point to Laurel and Violet Terraces (top); Primrose, Myrtle, Ivy and Daisy Terraces (middle); and Ivy Terrace (bottom).
The early Shaftesbury terraces and undeveloped land are further south, bounded by the Caledonian Railway. The substantial villas of Merchiston lie to the east beyond the Union Canal.

9.4 North Merchiston, Violet Terrace

migration of industry along the Fountainbridge-Dalry-Slateford axis during the last third of the nineteenth century. This industrial migration drew on the services, components suppliers, and infrastructure that earlier had supported the North British Rubber Company and the Scottish Vulcanite Rubber Company which together turned Edinburgh and Fountainbridge specifically into a world-leading centre of production for water-proofed shoes and sheets, and for clothing supplies to the army and navy, as well as industrial belts, shock absorbers and vulcanised rubber products.

Note: St Michael's Church was built on land sub-feued by the ECBC.

In just two years, 1878 and 1879, 56 new houses were built, sold, and occupied at North Merchiston. 'Considering the extraordinary state of the country and scarcity of money owing to the long continued commercial depression' this was considered 'very satisfactory' by the ECBC chairman in his Annual Report.[9] The 'extraordinary state' was a reference to the disastrous collapse of the City of Glasgow Bank in 1878 and the knock-on effects which resulted in the bankruptcy of two-thirds of all Glasgow builders,

9.5 McVitie & Price St Andrew's Biscuit Factory, Gorgie

Factory was situated across Slateford Road from Flowers and Shaftesbury Park Colonies

Source: Reproduced with permission of the National Railway Museum, Euston Collection, 1997-7409_LMS_3258

Note: Founded 1830 in Rose Street, moved to Stewart Terrace, Gorgie 1881 near Flowers and Shaftesbury Colonies, destroyed by fire, rebuilt 1894, and active until 1969. 'Digestive' biscuit introduced in 1892. Wedding cake for Princess Elizabeth and Lieutenant Philip Mountbatten 1947.

the failure of the City of Glasgow Improvement Trust, and more than a little anxiety in the Edinburgh building industry.[10]

Early settlers, as the first occupants of this 'Flower' Colony might be called, were originally from 26 of the 33 Scottish counties. Their skill set was just as varied. There were 35 different occupations amongst 77 household heads in 1881, the most common of which were clerk (19%) and a mixture of building trades (13%).[11] With an average age of 39, household heads had by that age normally undergone an apprenticeship or undertaken several years of training to acquire a measure of job security and predictable earnings. Women accounted for 13% of all household heads and almost all were reliant on fixed incomes (annuities) to afford their Colony property. Ten years later, in 1891, the number of 'Flowers' Colony homes had doubled to 154 with just over 700 residents and an average household size of 4.6 persons.

Between 1861 and 1881, that is, during its first twenty years, the ECBC enjoyed considerable success. Eight sites were acquired, almost 1,400 homes were built at an average of 55 per annum, and only 29 remain unsold. The logistics of such a scale of building work were impressive, to say the least, and a very considerable achievement since bankruptcy rather than longevity was a feature of the Victorian building industry nationally.

Perhaps the most significant indicator of ECBC achievements, however, was longevity of a different kind. Life expectancy was longer in Colony housing than in the city overall. Put differently, mortality in Colony housing was between a quarter and a third lower than the city-wide average (Fig. 9.6). Mortality levels were linked to Colony design. Separate households had separate front doors – tenements excepted – so this 'social distancing' insulated inhabitants of Colony houses against some of the hazards of infectious diseases. Well-being was also fostered by external design features. Self-contained sites bounded by railway lines and 'dead-end' roads encouraged children's games and fostered neighbourly interactions. Small, individual garden plots provided another focus of interest, and still does.

Home ownership itself also contributed to stability and continuity amongst Colony residents, and there were sufficient areas of both overlap and diversity in employment for workplace experiences to provide a forum for dialogue. Internal design, specifically, the provision of a kitchen sink, range, and WC, were also positive influences on the health of Colony residents and in sharp contrast to many tenement flats. Most importantly perhaps, price, whether in terms of mortgages or rent, defined the social and occupational composition and facilitated stability amongst Colony residents, as did continuity of management and the ongoing involvement of individual founder members.

In 1883 the ECBC faced another cliff edge in terms of new building. North Merchiston's Daisy Terrace was finished and ten properties in Lily Terrace were nearing completion. The modest cushion provided by Barnton Terrace was no longer available; all properties there were completed and rented. Just in time the ECBC obtained a 10-acre field from the Merchant Company in 1884 and almost immediately began work on twenty houses across the

Happy Homes

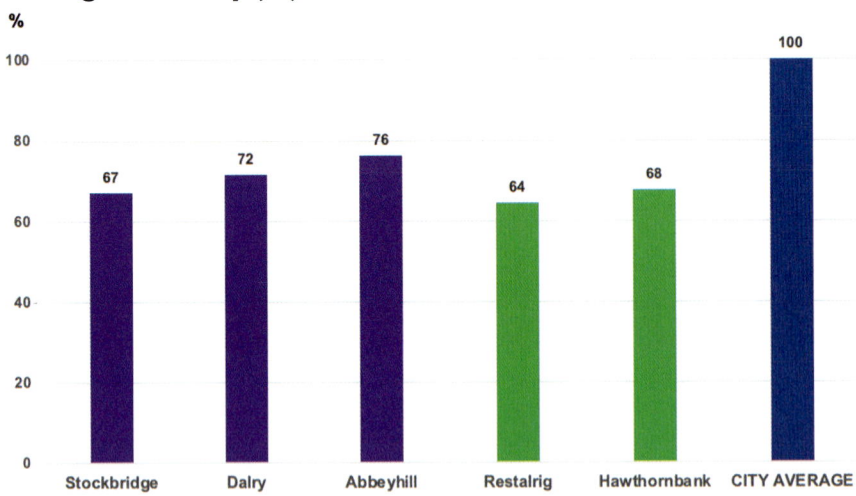

9.6 Mortality in Colonies Housing compared to Edinburgh or Leith Average Mortality (%)

Location	%
Stockbridge	67
Dalry	72
Abbeyhill	76
Restalrig	64
Hawthornbank	68
CITY AVERAGE	100

Source: NRS GD1/777/2, ECBC 24th Annual Report, May 1885.

railway tracks from Lily Terrace in what became Ashley Terrace in Shaftesbury Park – a double doffing of the cap to Lord Ashley, 7th Lord Shaftesbury. Had the deal with the Merchant Company been completed a year earlier then Shaftesbury Park, too, would have been outside the city limits, but a boundary extension in 1882 brought the area within Edinburgh with all the advantages of public amenities and urban management that that entailed.

The ECBC houses at Shaftesbury Park had access to the western entrance of Merchiston station and were 'conveniently situated for the suburban railway and the tramways'.[12] Three further signs of the Company's desire to appeal to a lower middle-class market were, firstly, more generous accommodation; secondly, 'four in a row' doors which gave access to the upper floor flat from doors that were indistinguishable from their neighbour's ground floor door (see Fig. 9.8); and thirdly, a greater degree of privacy since back extensions and boundary walls protected the rear gardens from prying eyes in a way that was impossible on previous developments.

Building Phases

9.7 Floor Plan Ashley Terrace, Shaftesbury Park

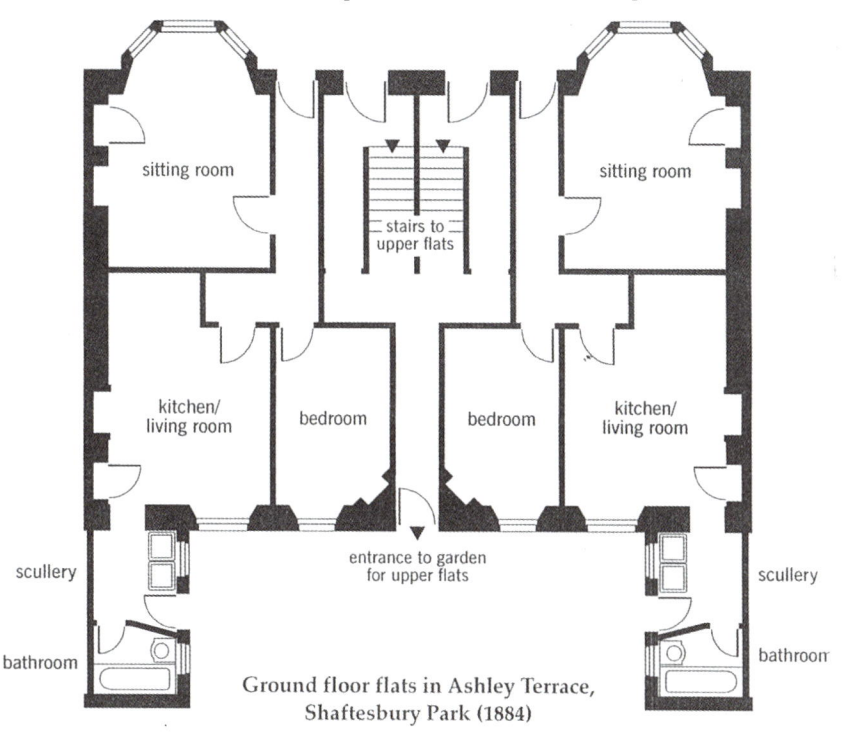

Ground floor flats in Ashley Terrace, Shaftesbury Park (1884)

9.8 Four Doors

A distinctive ECBC maisonette style at Shaftesbury Park, Hermitage Hill and Balgreen was copied elsewhere by private builders

109

A Change of Emphasis

For almost 30 years, in fact from the formation of the ECBC until his retirement in 1890 aged 69 on grounds of ill-health and old age, James Colville managed all the Company building sites.[13] Normally there were at least two, sometimes three and occasionally four sites active simultaneously. Colville's craft credentials as a stonemason and his role as President of the Masons' Union stood him in good stead when managing the day-to-day activities of the ECBC building sites. From his Stockbridge Colony home, first at 32 Bell Place and then at 16 Kemp Place, Colville walked at least 8 miles daily in the late-1860s and 1870s on his circuit of the Restalrig, Abbeyhill, and Dalry building sites before returning to the Company's yard at Stockbridge. Eventually, though not at the first asking, the Directors acknowledged Colville's age and commitment and allowed him a pony and trap.

Before his retirement, however, James Colville presided over a reorientation of ECBC activity. From 1883 the ECBC was committed to re-directing its activities towards new occupational groups at Shaftesbury Park. No longer were the building trades, printers, cabinetmakers, and railway workers the majority occupations amongst the ECBC homeowners. Artisans were still encouraged but the targets were different occupational groups – grocers and merchants, agents, clerical and administrative officers, and annuitants – whose regular salaries and pensions permitted more generous patterns of consumption, including higher rents. Overall, these social and occupational groups accounted for 76% of householders in Shaftesbury Park in 1891 – exactly double the average for the Colonies overall.

Colville's successor, George Mill, a joiner originally from Forfarshire, lived for several years in the model dwellings at Patriot Hall, Hamilton Place and had a background in the Cooperative movement. When in 1890 Mill assumed his managerial role Shaftesbury Park had been the only active ECBC building site since 1884. It was a marked change to the earlier Company strategy of overlapping projects. Also, no doubt with more than a little concern, the ECBC Directors issued a circular to shareholders urging them to bring the latest development 'to the notice of their friends' and to stress that Shaftesbury Park (Fig. 9.3) was 'unsurpassed' for its 'situation, convenience, moderate price and high-class workmanship'.[14] There was a general sense of foreboding.

With low turnover an issue, the ECBC Directors explained why they consciously decided to slow development at Shaftesbury Park:

> 'There has been so much property erected in that neighbourhood (Shandon area) during the past year or two that the directors have deemed it advisable not to push on building operations too fast, and thus grow a large quantity of property on to the market but have preferred to go on quietly with just as many houses as they thought were likely to be taken up.'[15]

Two economic principles were in conflict. Flooding the market with new homes would suppress house prices. On the other hand, economic theory suggested that 'supply creates its own demand' (Say's Law) and which seemed to be confirmed in the initial phases since ECBC homes sold almost as quickly as they were completed, Trafalgar Street flats excepted. A prompt turnover of property also meant that the ECBC received a capital injection from sales and was released from the overhead costs of taxes and land charges (feu duties). But from the mid-1880s the number of unsold ECBC houses began to increase. The ECBC was between a rock and a hard place. The managerial strategy was to avoid flooding the market with new houses which is why the Directors decided to slow production at Shaftesbury. What they overlooked was the fact that they could not control other builders, and the overall supply of new homes.

Whereas in the first 25 years multiple sites were in different stages of development, in 1890 the Company had just a single income stream – Shaftesbury. In 1891, 10 houses at Hollybank Terrace were completed, 8 were in progress, and 18 under consideration with the planning authority, the Dean of Guild Court. This level of completions was just one fifth that of the annual average of the 1860 and 1870s.

How far Colville's day-to-day managerial nous was affected by his age and declining health, or whether it was the ageing David Rintoul (Chairman, foreman mason until 1893, and ECBC founder member) or David R. Kemp (long time Treasurer) that lacked vigour and foresight at this critical time in the ECBC's history is difficult to say. Mill's relative inexperience may also have been a factor. The ECBC's exposed position in 1890 was almost certainly influenced by a sequence of difficult years in the housebuilding industry nationally during 1885, 1886 and 1887. As the shareholders heard at the AGM in 1886, 'For the last few years the building trade in Edinburgh has not been in a very prosperous condition', and in 1887 they were again reminded of 'the continued general depression in trade throughout the country'.[16] The Directors' comment that, notwithstanding these circumstances, the year 1887 was 'very satisfactory' is baffling, if nothing else. Each of the ten years 1883 to 1892 was by far the worst experienced to date by the ECBC.

A single building site was potentially catastrophic for the ECBC for at least two reasons: first, the skilled workforce familiar with ECBC designs and standards might melt away; and second, the company was exposed to fixed charges on land but lacked a steady revenue stream to meet them from sites at different stages of development. It is no exaggeration that the acquisition of land at Hermitage Hill in 1891 adjoining the ECBC's existing Restalrig Park site was considered 'the most important transaction' of the year.[17] However, acquisition of land was one thing: completion of buildings was another. The ECBC failed to complete any new housing at Hermitage Hill in time for the crucial point in the year (Martinmas) when tenants sought to renew rental agreements or embark on a house purchase. Whether unfinished, unsold, or unlet property was left in ECBC hands.

There were, indeed, stresses and strains within the organisation. One persistent source of tension was over the issue of the annual dividend. Should profits be set aside as Reserves for a 'rainy day', or, distributed as higher dividends to demonstrate the ECBC's commercial success and appeal to shareholders? As one shareholder succinctly observed: 'there is nothing divine but dividends.' But such a 'grab', D. W. Kemp claimed, would mean that 'reserves would soon go to swell dividends'. The Committee concluded that the objective was for 'the investment of more of the shareholders own money in their own business instead of scattering the funds in large dividends,' and in 1899 strongly urged the chairman, Andrew Salmond, and the Board of Directors 'to considerably add to the reserves'.[18]

9.9 Hazelbank and Shaftesbury Terraces

PHOTO: John Reiach

To improve their cash flow the ECBC Directors occasionally sold on elements of their property interests. This was the case in 1880 with the easternmost wedge of land at North Merchiston, sold for £500 to the Trustees of a new church (St Michael's) on Slateford Road, and again in 1902 when the Caledonian Railway paid £554 for a small portion of Shaftesbury Park. In 1904, 'after deliberation', the Company also sold their rights to ground charges (feu duties) on 310 houses in Shaftesbury Park for £3,159 following an agreement reached with the Trustees of the Widows' Fund of the Merchants of the City of Edinburgh. These transactions prompted another financial initiative, a feu duty redemption account, established in 1913, where buy-outs of feu duties improved the liquidity of the ECBC.[19]

The mid-1890s were years of managed success with the ECBC building in a controlled way at both Shaftesbury Park and Hermitage Hill.[20] Fronting the Shaftesbury development was Ashley Terrace, after which Hazelbank and Hollybank Terraces were completed (Fig.9.3). The builders then moved progressively if cautiously westward on the site to develop terraces at Almondbank (1895-1902), Briarbank (1896-97) and, furthest from the main road, Alderbank Terrace, Place, and Gardens (1900-05).

At Hermitage Hill lands acquired by the Company in 1891 were described in promotional literature as 'unrivalled in Leith or vicinity' for beauty. Cornhill Terrace was planned in 1892 and finished in 1897; four houses in East Restalrig Terrace were also underway in 1892 and others were gradually added until 1910. Four houses were shoe-horned into a plot in 1892 in Summerfield Place on land previously developed by W. & A. Fingzies and the Industrial Cooperative Building Company.[21] The sequence of housebuilding then continued at Ryehill Terrace which was completed by 1898 when building activity moved to Ryehill Place, Gardens and Avenue from 1899 to 1906, with those fronting Restalrig Road spanning the years 1906-14. By 1914, 360 homes had been built, rented or sold, at Hermitage Hill rivalling the Stockbridge Colony with 379 and exceeding Shaftesbury where 330 homes were built.

The synchronicity of both the scale and timing in the Shaftesbury and Hermitage Hill developments is striking. Though the first few

Building Phases

9.10 Hermitage Hill

Source: Reproduced with the permission of the NLS OS 1933

190 Hermitage Hill houses separated those of the ECBC to the south at Restalrig Park, and others to north, built by the Industrial Cooperative Building Company (A. & W. Fingzies).

115

Shaftesbury years were uneven, both it and the Hermitage Hill developments were very much in step thereafter. Both peaked in 1899 with steady and pronged expansion beforehand followed by an almost uninterrupted decline to 1912 after a secondary peak (1902-03). The annual average of homes built was also roughly similar in both areas, as was the overall scale with 330 ECBC homes at Shaftesbury Park and 360 at Hermitage Hill.

The ECBC's performance in the 1890s and 1900s was in keeping with broader national trends in housebuilding, and more specifically, with the overall pattern in Edinburgh where the peak year was 1898 (Fig. 9.11). With land at Shaftesbury Park almost fully exploited, and that at Hermitage finite, hemmed in as it was by the pre-existing Restalrig Park and the Fingzies Industrial Road development, a further site was considered essential by the ECBC Directors.

On Christmas eve 1902 the ECBC concluded an agreement with Sir William James Gardiner Baird (1854-1921), 8th Baronet of Saughtonhall for 9.364 acres of his Saughtonhall estate.[22] It was a shrewd acquisition. Like the flat flood plain of the Water of Leith at the Stockbridge site, Saughton was a remnant of the ancient Corstorphine Loch, and thus even and easily worked. Like Shaftesbury Park, and consistent with the practice of 'Colony' building at the urban fringe, the area had been incorporated into the city of Edinburgh just six years earlier and so had the advantage of a greenfield site. Fortuitously, Baird's land was also the location of a privately run mental asylum which passed to Edinburgh Corporation in 1906 and subsequently became the site of the Scottish National Exhibition in 1908. This attracted 125,000 visitors on the opening day – 1st May 1908 – and 3.5 million people six months later when the Exhibition ended. There can be little doubt that the Exhibition put Balgreen and Saughton on the map for many Edinburgh citizens.

The dotted line in Fig. 9.13 marks the extended municipal boundary, with new ECBC housing development visible on Saughtonhall Drive, Balgreen Road and Avenue, and Glendevon Place. Physically, the Balgreen site possessed some of the trademark ECBC features: a railway line on two sides of a quadrilateral, the Water of Leith on a third side, while the 'Stank' – an underground conduit – marked a fourth boundary. Pinkhill

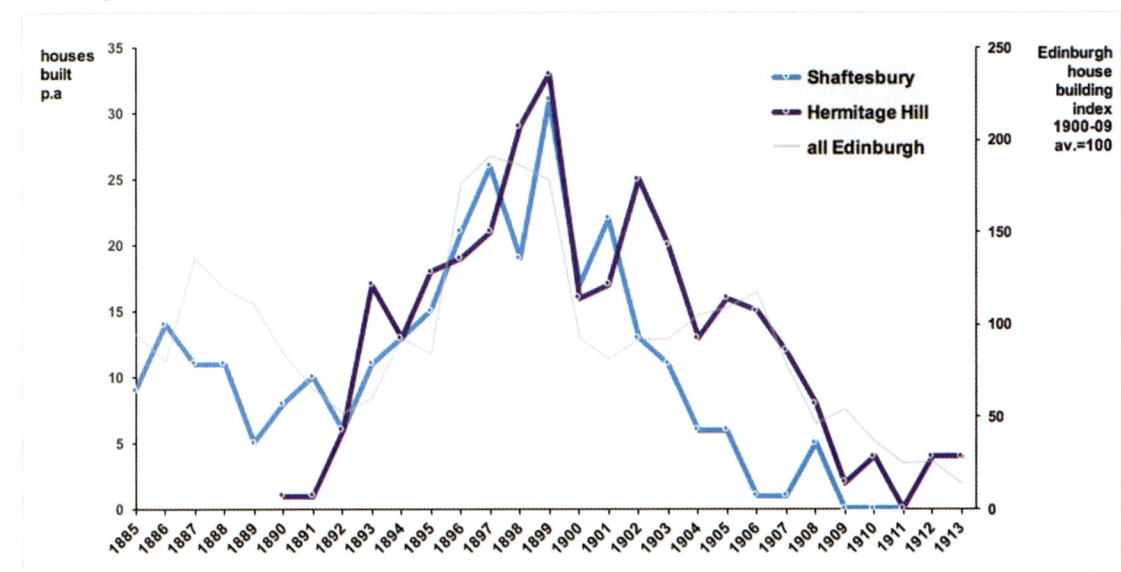

9.11 Synchronicity: ECBC Housebuilding at Shaftesbury Park and Hermitage Hill

station, opened in 1902, offered rail access on the west, and the tram terminus when extended to Western Corner connected with Saughtonhall Avenue. Unusually for the ECBC, therefore, there were several nodes of concurrent development *within* the Balgreen site.

Source: ECBC Annual Reports 1885-1913; Edinburgh City Archives, SL144/24/7 & 8, Dean of Guild Court, Register of Plans 1885-1913.

The acquisition of land at Balgreen was both perceptive and timely as far as the ECBC was concerned. It also re-established the pattern of an overlapping chronology, a form generational progression as sites went from infancy to maturity to decline in terms of their exploitation. Just four months after the land transfer with the Baird family was concluded, that is, by May 1903, six continuous villas akin to those at East Restalrig Terrace, Hermitage Hill were 'in the course of erection' and eight others proposed 'of a similar class to those built at Shaftesbury Park'.[23] Even if house design was tried and tested a new century appeared to usher in a new era for the ECBC at Balgreen.

In the following decades, the Balgreen site developed significantly with 187 houses built and occupied.[24] There was a cluster of 80 ECBC homes facing each other in Glendevon Place which backed on to another substantial Colony of Company homes on Balgreen Road. There were also ECBC construction sites on three other streets – Balgreen Avenue and Saughton Crescent which were at some distance from one another – and Saughtonhall Drive.

Happy Homes

Scottish National Exhibition, Edinburgh, 1908

9.12 The Saughton site of the International Exhibition, 1908
postcard unearthed during excavations on the Royal College of Surgeons site. Reproduced by permisssion of RCSEd.

However, a fundamental shift in ECBC activities took place at Balgreen. Previously, indeed for its entire existence, the ECBC had feued (acquired) land, built property on it, and then sold or rented the houses, thus relieving the Company of the land charges. Not long after the Balgreen land was obtained from the Baird family, housebuilding activity in Edinburgh went into steep decline. Warrants (permits) for new housing in the city declined year on year from 1906 to 1914 (see 9.11 grey line).[25] Only four houses at Balgreen were finished in 1910. On the 50th anniversary of the foundation of the ECBC in 1911 the Directors nostalgically reported that land released by the removal of the building yard from Stockbridge to Annandale Street enabled the Company to build and sell six houses on the original Stockbridge site, 'thus completing the earliest feuing venture on the Company.'[26] These were the only houses completed by the ECBC in 1911. With depression in the building trade unabated in 1912 and 1913, the Annual Report stated that 'directors deem it wise to suspend operations meantime.'[27] Even before the outbreak of World War I ECBC housebuilding was at a standstill.

While external factors, such as the general state of the housebuilding industry, were important to the ECBC's activities it was largely for internal financial reasons that the Balgreen development marked a change of emphasis. As with any producer, a proportion of output remained unsold and so the ECBC was obliged to function as a

Building Phases

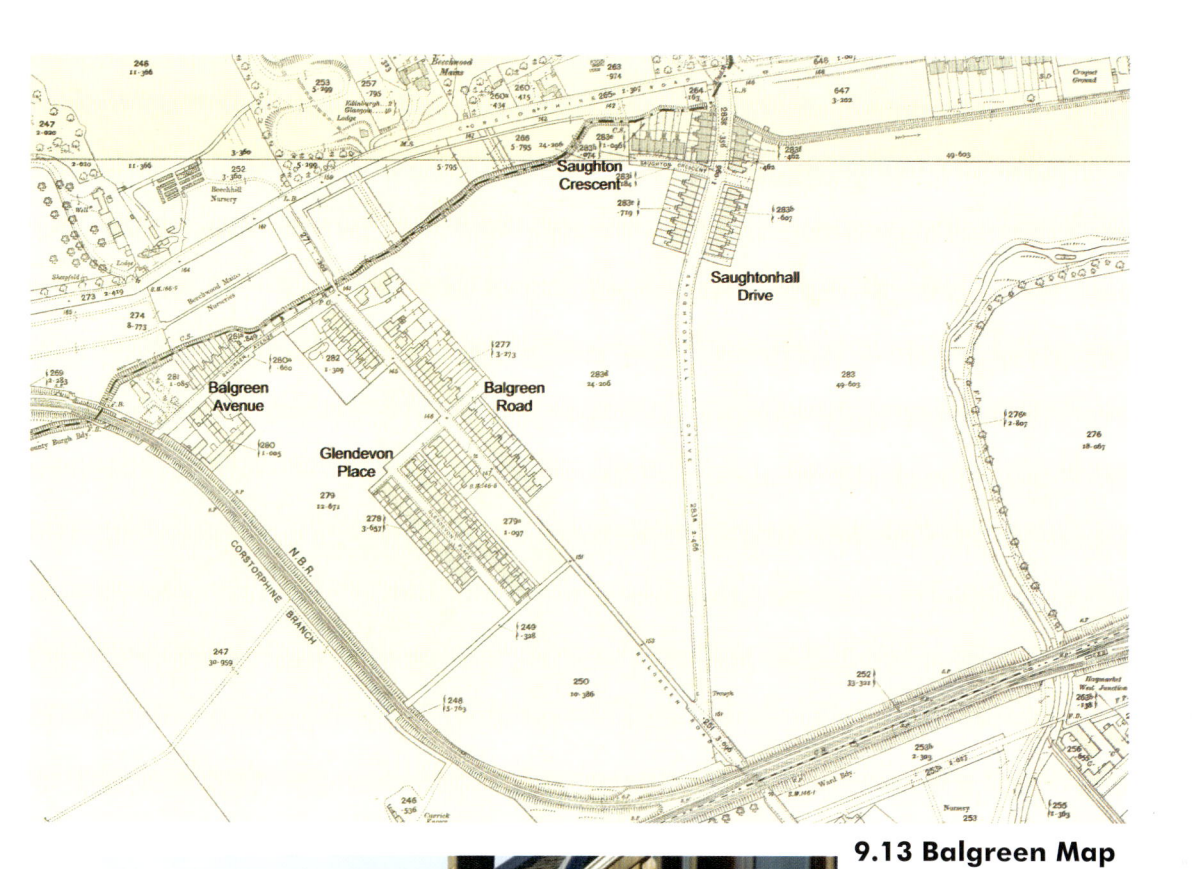

9.13 Balgreen Map

9.14 Glendevon Place

119

9.15 Unsold ECBC Housing Stock 1865-1914

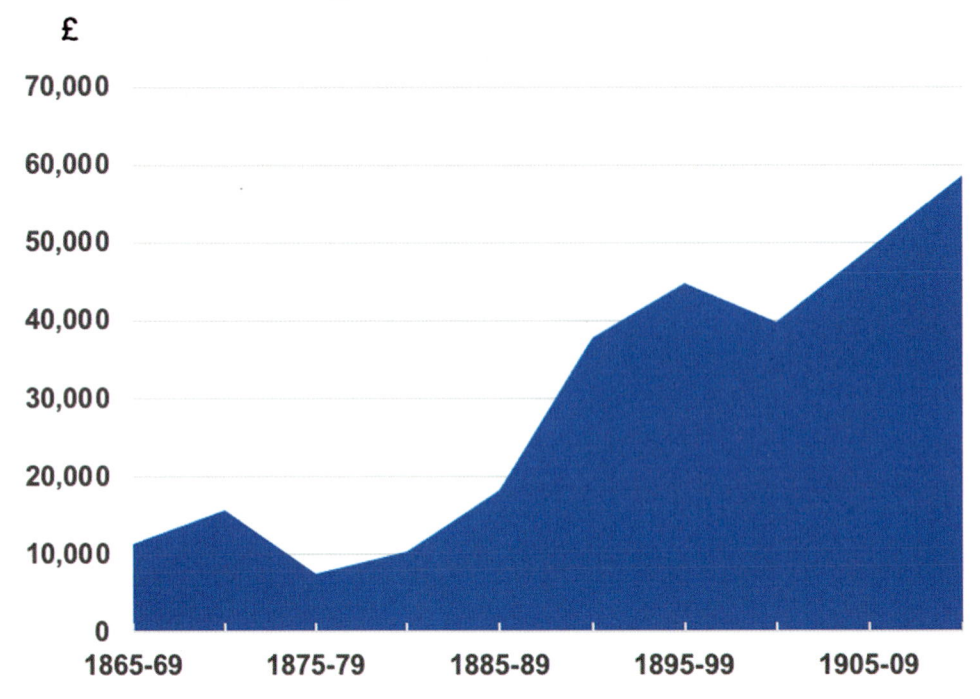

Source: NRS GD488 Annual Reports 1865-1914

landlord and to address its excess stocks. Until the 1880s the extent of this unsold property was roughly equivalent to the value of annual house sales, but in the late-1880s and early-1890s the ratio of unsold to sold properties quadrupled. The situation deteriorated further, and faster, after 1907 with unsold property at least nine times that of house sales. It was an untenable position for the Company. As a landlord, capital was tied up. The turnover of capital was so slow that the ECBC's function as a builder of 'Happy Homes' for working families was compromised.

It was the balance sheet, therefore, that disproportionately influenced the ECBC strategy in the twentieth century. With a surfeit of unsold property there was an incentive for the Company to curtail construction and become more of a developer and factor than builder, selling off plots of land in Balgreen Road and Saughtonhall Drive to builders John Duncan and John Armstrong amongst others, and to the Suburban Feuing Company whose agents were Simpson & Marwick WS.

Compared to the Hermitage Hill development of Ryehill and Cornhill streets before 1914 where the ECBC retained only 10% of the properties for renting, the ECBC had become house factors and letting agents at Balgreen rather than builders. As a result, rather than the homogeneous suburban appearance of Hermitage Hill and Shaftesbury Park the ECBC brand was compromised by a variety of others at Balgreen, the last of its developments. A critical factor, however, was the overhang of unsold houses which deterred the ECBC from engagement with a new political world and the socio-economic conditions of twentieth century Britain.

Happy Homes

External stairs at Stockbridge Colonies

PHOTO: John Reiach

10. War, Depression and Decline

THE POOR physical condition of army recruits was a matter of national concern during the Boer War (1899-1902) and a considerable volume of anthropometric data was subsequently collected regarding the state of the nation's health. In Edinburgh, for example, in 1904 the Charity Organisation Society examined the average age-specific heights of children from Broughton School, an essentially lower-middle class area, and compared them with those attending North Canongate School, a poorer part of the Old Town. The Broughton children were between one and three inches taller.[1] Convincing statistical evidence from Glasgow and Dundee corroborated this correlation between health and housing standards. National concern for the physical state of the population and the defence of the realm informed clauses in the Education Acts, 1906 and 1907 which empowered local authorities to provide free school meals and medical inspections. Ominously for the ECBC, perhaps, Edinburgh Corporation intervened in the housing market by using funds from the Public Works Loan Board to construct council housing and by 1913 accommodation for over 600 families was available at Tynecastle, the Cowgate and West Port.[2]

When the Board of Trade Price Index (1900=100) rose from 117 in 1914 to 144 in 1915 rents, as a major component of household budgets, became a major political issue during the First World War. 'Rent Strikes' and 'Red Clydeside' gained political leverage.[3] In response, the wartime British government promptly introduced the Rent Restrictions Act, 1915 which, with some relaxation, continued until 1957. Intended to placate tenants, inevitably this freeze on wartime rents significantly undermined the long run rental incomes of private individuals, and of the ECBC which had become a landlord rather than a housebuilder.

With wartime housebuilding already suspended and rents controlled the ECBC was adversely affected by a third development. The Liberal Party's election pledge in 1919 to subsidise a public housing programme – 'Homes Fit for Heroes' – created a template for state intervention in the housing market. This was a short-lived two-year initiative, suspended in 1921 as the Treasury sought to gain tighter monetary control.

The 'Addison' Housing Act, 1919, as it was known, was replaced with different subsidy arrangements under the Conservative Government's Housing Act, 1923. Centralised control was replaced by local authority management with a Treasury contribution of £6 p.a. per house for twenty years. But the particularly innovative element was for a Treasury lump sum payment of £75 to building firms on completion of a private sector house. Local authorities were also permitted to make extra funding available to lend money to builders, and to underwrite loans made by building societies. Thus, owner occupiers were subsidised from central taxation; builders' risks were minimised by local council guarantees. A year later, in 1924, a Labour Government Housing Act (Wheatley) increased the subsidy to builders and, crucially, re-established local councils' powers to provide houses for the working classes without, as previously, being required to show that private enterprise was unable to supply them.

In the 1920s there were 15% fewer insured building workers in Scotland than elsewhere in Britain, and in Edinburgh the net output per building worker compared unfavourably with every

Source: Edinburgh Corporation Treasurer's Committee Minutes 1923-34, reproduced in A. O'Carroll, 'Social homes, private houses', p.219.

Table 10.1 Subsidised Private Building Firms in Edinburgh 1923-34

	name of builder	number of houses
1	James Miller	1922
2	T. S. Henderson	203
3	G. R. Black	96
4	Bangholm Building Company	90
5	Ford and Torrie	89
6	Edinburgh Suburban Building Society	88
7	C. H. Dunlop	86
8	R. J. Robinson	83
9	Blyth Building Company	73
10	Anderson and Walker	68

other area of Scotland, England, and Wales.[4] Lack of mechanisation and an over-reliance on manual labour and traditional craft skills in small firms were characteristic of the Edinburgh building industry. The Housing Acts of 1923 and 1924 provided financial tools that stimulated activity amongst private builders. Around 3,000 houses were built under the terms of the 1923 Act and 6,500 under the 1924 Act.[5] The result was that three-quarters of all private sector housing in Edinburgh between 1918 and 1932 was built with the financial assistance of Edinburgh Corporation.[6] In the years 1919-39, local authorities in Scotland subsidised and built 68% of all new homes; private enterprise built 32%. In England the percentages were reversed: 28% public and 72% private.

What distinguished housing policy in Edinburgh in the interwar years and until the 1960s, therefore, was the preference of a dominant 'Progressive' alliance in the Housing Committee (Conservative, Liberal and Independent councillors, including Protestant Action) for subsidies to builders of private homes for both rent and ownership.[7] This fundamentally shifted the context of housebuilding for the ECBC.

Why the ECBC was not party to the Edinburgh Corporation's subsidies to private builders remains unclear. Conceivably its Cooperative credentials might have been a compromising factor given the political complexion of the Housing Committee. Another possible explanation is that the ECBC simply did not apply or, more likely, that it no longer had the working capital or the workforce – or both – to undertake housebuilding projects on a sufficient scale and so was not approved at the application stage for a financial subsidy from the Corporation.

Another explanation for the inactivity of the ECBC after World War I lies in complacency and the directors' tendency to assign blame for the decline of Company exclusively to external factors – the post-war conditions, economic uncertainty, and controlled rents during the war. ECBC shareholders were informed in 1920 about the Company's 'happy position' of having a stock of 200 completed pre-war houses for sale. Insulated by this stock of unsold assets, the ECBC directors built very little housing after 1919 and relied heavily on occasional sales and mostly on rental incomes from unsold stock. It was on this basis that the directors were able to announce a dividend of at least 10% to shareholders in every year after 1922 – more than double the rate of interest or yields in the bond market. In short, with such levels of assured 'unearned' income and the British economy voluntarily pursuing deflationary measures why, the directors reasoned, should they embark on risky housebuilding ventures even supposing they had the capacity?

It is difficult to escape the conclusion that the demise of the ECBC was not simply due to a wartime hiatus but more to longer term managerial failings already evident at the dawn of a new century. A critique of the business model had been advanced as early as 1901. In a letter to Chairman Andrew Salmond, D.W. Kemp explained that the Directors offered little or no forward planning for the ECBC:

> '(N)early all the directors are wage-earners (no disrespect) and have had no experience whatever in carrying on a business. . . it would seem that the duty of a director of our Company is simply to hurrah! hurrah!'[8]

He continued:

> 'We have not been making much or anything on our buildings for some years – we have been subsisting on the past. We have for years been imperceptibly adding improvements all costing money – in fact producing beautiful residences – but the Company has been getting no adequate return for the expenditure.'

The ECBC was also inflexible in relation to its house designs. Methods and materials were also undergoing change and the Chairman and directors commented disparagingly about the quality and design of post-war housing in Edinburgh:

> 'The vast number of houses of the Bungalow type which have sprung up. . . in all parts of the suburbs have created a craze which is militating against the demand for the Company's more [staid but infinitely more] substantially built property.'
> (Note: The words in square brackets were struck from his speech)

The ECBC was content to claim that 'the market was acting adversely' and would return to its senses. Perversely, the directors

10.1 Miller Homes: Davidson Road Bungalow

felt sure that 'when the Bungalow production reaches its zenith the reaction toward the company's class of house will be apparent'. This optimism, that there was 'still hope for recovery of stone-built housing', was misplaced. Private housing estates were colonising suburbia. In England the ubiquitous semi-detached villas of the 1930s were the physical manifestation of a house-building boom generated by 'cheap money' as interest rates plummeted following the financial crises of 1929-31. In eight months borrowing costs fell from 6% in September 1931 to 2% in June 1932. In the Scottish cities, for 'semi-detached' craze read 'bungalow'.

Nor did the ECBC seem to appreciate structural changes in demand. The growth in white-collar office work in the inter-war period should have been particularly obvious to the ECBC since so many of their Victorian housing developments were populated by clerical grades. Few organisations, if any, were better placed to understand the merits a mortgage scheme that relied fundamentally on steady employment and predictable pay.

In Edinburgh, the composition of employment insulated its inhabitants from the worst effects of international depression in the inter-war years. It was a city with the highest proportion of professional workers in Britain and, related to this, a steady level of employment for skilled workers in the consumption trades. Annuitants living on legacies and other retirees were also heavily represented. Compared to most other towns or cities, therefore, the levels of income and wealth in Edinburgh in the inter-war years meant that demand was relatively buoyant for house and car ownership, as it was for the purchase of radios, vacuum cleaners, and other appliances associated with the widespread introduction of electricity to the home. Some building firms responded positively to the new opportunities, but the ECBC was unable to recognise the long-run changes in demand. Instead, the Company retained a faith in the eventual return to stone-built houses of the pre-1914 type.

Risk avoidance, therefore, was the organising principle of ECBC activities in the inter-war years. House sales reached double figures – though only just – in three years, 1923-25. Building operations, suspended during the War, were barely resumed. Whereas in its pomp, the ECBC had itself employed over 200 workmen and sub-contracted work to other firms, by the 1920s and throughout the 1930s a skeleton workforce was engaged only on repair and maintenance work and their wages amounted to less than the office staff who administered the Company. So distanced had the ECBC become in the inter-war period from the construction of new houses that it bought no new sites and sold off part of its undeveloped Balgreen property in 1934, ironically to a builder, C. H. Dunlop, in receipt of subsidies from Edinburgh Corporation. The directors openly contemplated giving up housebuilding altogether and functioning only as a building society.

The ECBC slid into insignificance. So infrequent was its house-building that it lacked the labour force and management systems ever again to undertake building on any scale. The Company limped on by retaining and renting 50 of its Colony houses in 1943 with a book value of £26,000 (see Appendix 3).[9] The balance sheet also showed a small loss. World War II only confirmed what was already apparent and in 1945 a restructuring took place with a capital injection intended to kick-start the business which was re-badged as Edinburgh Building Contractors Ltd. Post-war shortages of building materials posed problems for the Company which were not assisted by the severe winter of 1947 so that by

1948 the decline in contracting business seriously reduced revenue. Dividends fell to 2.5% – the lowest ever in ninety years. Contract tenders were submitted for extensions to Eyemouth and Selkirk Schools, for kitchens at Galashiels Academy, work on Spylaw House for Edinburgh Corporation and a Research Institute at Roslin. But these came to little and only showed how far the Company had moved away from housebuilding. Indeed, more than three-fifths of the Company's business came from jobbing work, minor house conversions and as income when acting as Master of Works on the contracts won by other housebuilding firms. The first ever loss was recorded in 1950, and 1951 was the worst year ever financially. Though the Company attempted in 1954 to shed its former difficulties through another change of name to E. B. Contractors Limited, it was unable to do so and at a special meeting the size of its liabilities forced a voluntary liquidation. It ceased to trade. The ECBC in its reincarnated corporate form, E. B. Contractors Limited, was finally dissolved on the 15th October 1970. It was an ignominious end to a path-breaking venture by a small visionary group of skilled tradesmen.

Happy Homes

PHOTO: John Reiach

Quiet contemplation in the centre of a modern city: Abbeyhill

11. Who Lived in the Colonies?

ONE OF THE ECBC's strongest supporters, Hugh Gilzean Reid, wrote of an imaginary couple, John Wilson and Mary Brown, soon to be wed and enjoying a stroll in the direction of Stockbridge.

'I have resolved' said John, 'never to take you to any of those dingy hovels off the High Street, or even to those barrack-like blocks.'

Mary replied: 'How horrible it must be to live in those dark closes and be forced to associate. . . with the people one sees there!' She was reminded of 'poor Mrs Smith' papering her 'dingy rooms' even though the rain would soon run down the walls, of the language of the drunken neighbours, and of the hostile conditions in which children grew up there.

John remarked 'I have been determined, with God's help, to commence life with you in other and better circumstances; and at last the possibility is placed within our reach.' He spoke of his purchase of twenty £1 shares in the Edinburgh Cooperative Building Company and his intention to buy a house in Reid Terrace.

Mary's incredulity was evident: 'John – you must be dreaming.'

John pointed out the actual spot they would occupy: 'It seems like a dream, but it is as much a reality as our wedding.' John commented, referring to the quality of building, amenities, separate entrance, and the mortgage arrangements.

The imaginary episode concluded with the reflection that, some years after their wedding, they had 'for a long period owned their house.'

Reid concluded: 'to all workers. . . the story is full of instruction and hope.'[1]

Hugh Gilzean-Reid focussed on 'the Poor' and 'Cooperation.' James Begg referred 'Happy Homes' and 'Working-Men'. If these were the intended beneficiaries were the objectives of the ECBC realised? Was it 'working men' who benefitted? Was Reid right to stress cooperation? And were the 'the poor' housed?

'Happy Homes' were located on the periphery of the city – the Colonies. They were initially affordable mainly because land was less pressurised, less precious at the urban fringe.[2] The earliest Colonies were developed on awkward marginal plots, hemmed in by railway lines and exposed to the noise and soot associated with them. A distinguishing feature was that ECBC houses were intended as – and generally were – family homes. Indeed, even the street names leeched 'family' status, grouped by the names of trees and plants at Restalrig, North Merchiston, Shaftesbury, and Hermitage Hill. ECBC developments were also given a collective identity by referring to them as a 'Park', as in Glenogle Park, Norton Park, North Merchiston Park, Shaftesbury Park, and Glendevon Park. In so doing the Company conveyed their various housing developments positively as related, part of a larger family, and having distinct and desirable identities with health, social and economic benefits that marked them out from other builders through their ECBC 'brand' and design features.

Grouped street names also evoked family values and community through cooperation and solidarity. Amongst the best known individuals nationally for these values, were the political figures of John Bright and Richard Cobden, radical supporters of working men's rights and commemorated in the names of the Dalry terraces. Locally supportive figures politically were Francis Brown Douglas, (Lord Provost 1859-62) a member of the steering group of Pilrig Model Dwellings; Duncan McLaren, MP (Lord Provost 1851-54; MP 1865-81) an ardent supporter of free education; and Councillors Lewis and Walker, an indomitable duo who spoke frequently and forcibly in the Town Council on housing and health issues as they affected labourers and their families.[3] Their significance was also enshrined in the names of the Dalry Colony streets. Others closely associated with the cooperative spirit of the founders – Reid, Miller, Rintoul, Colville, Collins, Kemp, and Bell – formed a 'family' of like-minded individuals, and their names and the tools of their building trades are embedded in the gable walls of Colony houses in Stockbridge and North Merchiston. Six Colonies have commemorative tablets to James Colville, sometimes in conjunction with a carved stone image of bees and beehives, which represented the work ethic and community values of the Cooperative movement nationally, and of which James Colville was an outstanding example. The Edinburgh 'Colonies' were, and are, full of symbolism.

The core ECBC design or 'brand' was not unchanging. From 1877 the distinctive external staircases were abandoned at North Merchiston, and front and rear access to the terraces ceased from 1884 at Shaftesbury Park. They were generally replaced with a quartet of four-in-a-row doors (see Fig. 9.8) with the inner pair providing access to 'upper doors' flats – a design feature subsequently copied by private builders elsewhere in the city, for example, at Kirkhill and Willowbrae. Attic rooms with dormer windows were used frequently in early ECBC developments to provide more intensive use of the plot footprint. The introduction of bay windows (North Merchiston) then became standard at Shaftesbury, Hermitage Hill, and Balgreen and so produced modest additional floor space, as did back extensions which were a response to broader societal changes in family living which increasingly distinguished between communal living space and private or personal space.

11.1 Duncan McLaren (1800-86)
Source: Duncan McLaren, Lord Provost 1851-54 reproduced with permission of the City Art Centre, Museums & Galleries Edinburgh. Artist: George Reid.

Real wages in Britain improved on average by 1.2% per annum between 1856 and 1899.[4] However this had more to do with falling prices than rising wages as international grain prices plummeted in the last quarter of the nineteenth century. This is not to claim that boom and bust were banished. Far from it. But for those in regular work falling prices facilitated an unprecedented and sustained improvement in their purchasing power and living standards, as reflected partly in the more spacious accommodation of the final three Colony developments – Shaftesbury, Hermitage Hill and Balgreen. By way of contrast, a study of over 22,000 households and 92,000 inhabitants in the closes and wynds of the Old Town between 1861 and 1891 revealed a reduction of 26% in the overall number of inhabitants but was accompanied by an 8% increase in the average household size.[5] The City Improvement Act, 1867 and the resulting tenement clearances came with a real penalty for those left behind, and not least through the deconstruction of support networks.

Happy Homes

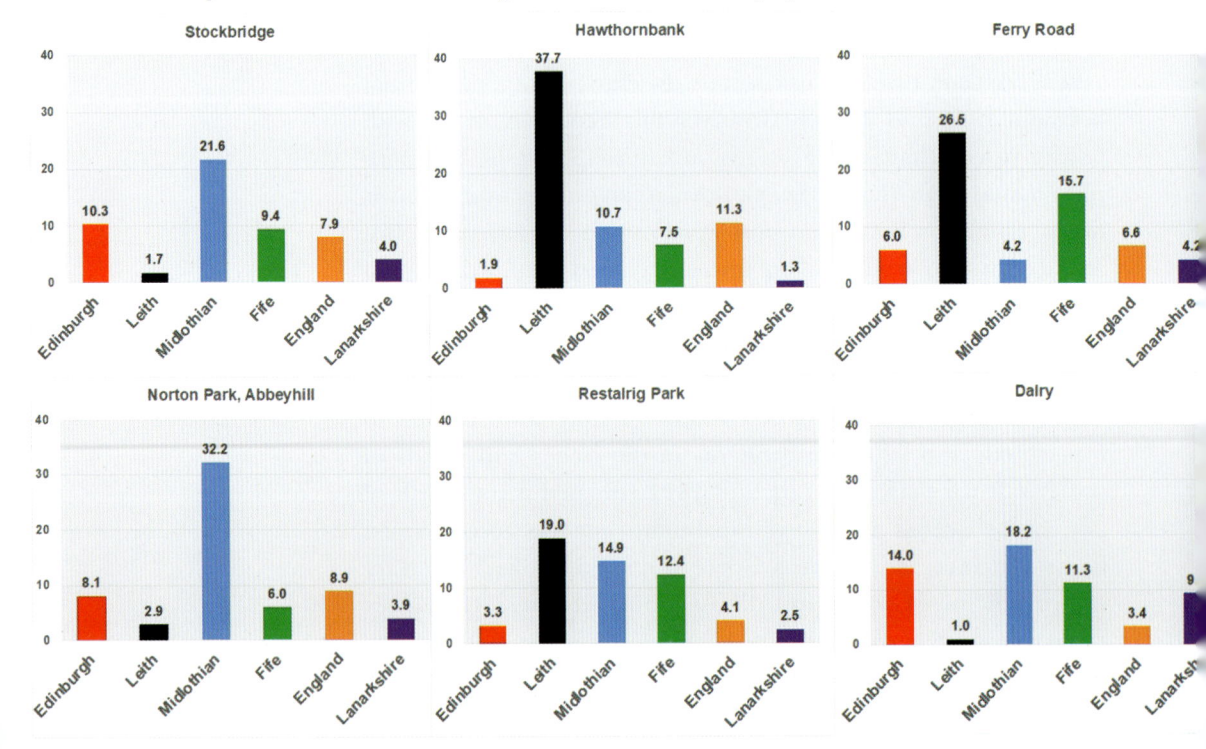

Table 11.1 Birthplaces of Adult Residents in Edinburgh Colonies, 1871 (%)

Bridge	Stock Bank (%)	Hawthorn Road (%)	Ferry Park (%)	Norton Park (%)	Restalrig (%)	Dalry 1871 (%)	all (%)
Midlothian	21.6	10.7	4.2	32.2	14.9	18.2	**20.9**
Edinburgh	10.3	1.9	6.0	8.1	3.3	14.0	**9.2**
Fife	9.4	7.5	15.7	6.0	12.4	11.3	**9.5**
England	7.9	11.3	6.6	8.9	4.1	3.4	**7.2**
Lanarkshire	4.0	1.3	4.2	3.9	2.5	9.4	**4.7**
Leith	1.7	37.7	26.5	2.9	19.0	1.0	**7.2**
top 6 areas	54.9	70.4	63.2	62.0	56.2	57.3	**58.7**
adult numbers	875	159	166	484	121	406	**2211**

Note: Lanarkshire and Perthshire both 4.7% overall in 1871.

11.2 Birthplaces of Adult Colony Residents, 1871 (%)

134

Who Lived in the Colonies?

Table 11.2 Birthplaces of Adult Residents in Edinburgh Colonies 1881-91 (%)

	North Merchiston 1881 (%)	Shaftesbury Park 1891 (%)	Hermitage Hill 1901 (%)	All 3 later colonies 1881-1901(%)
Midlothian*	5.6	8.0	7.6	**12.9**
Edinburgh*	27.6	18.0	12.8	**12.2**
Fife	5.6	9.3	5.6	**6.7**
England	9.2	11.9	6.4	**8.8**
Lanarkshire	10.8	11.0	4.3	**7.9**
Leith	0.4	1.2	31.1	**14.6**
top 6 areas	**59.2**	**70.4**	**63.2**	**62.5**
adult numbers	250	335	485	1070

Source: Census of Scotland, Edinburgh, 1871-1901

Note: Adult defined as over 13 as this eliminates children born in the Colonies.

*Estimate: Midlothian and Edinburgh not distinguished separately in 1881.

The 'Colonists'

By 1871, six ECBC Colonies had been established, and some completed. The birthplaces of the residents of these ECBC 'Happy Homes' were often far flung. Indeed, adults born in every Scottish county migrated to these six Colonies, though eighteen counties each contributed fewer than 1% of adult Colony residents, and collectively totalled only 9% in the six developments established in the 1860s. The migrations were fewest from those born in Bute, Nairn, Dunbarton, Sutherland and Wigton, though in reality there was little to separate these eighteen counties. Irish and 'foreign' born constituted 1-2% of Colony residents, mostly in Stockbridge, and those born in Roxburgh, Caithness, and Berwickshire experienced a disproportionate exodus given their own rather modest county populations.

Revealing patterns can be identified from the birthplaces of more than 3,300 adult Colony residents. Indeed, the same six geographical areas provided the highest percentage of birthplaces in each of nine Colonies and in each of four Censuses – 1871, 1881, 1891, and 1901 – though the ranking within the top six birthplaces differed.[6] The six birthplaces which contributed the highest percentages of Colony residents were in order: 1. Midlothian 2. Fife 3. Edinburgh 4. Leith and England 6. Lanarkshire (Tables 11.1 and 11.2).

In the three Leith Colonies localism was particularly strong with Hawthornbank (38%), Ferry Road (27%) and Restalrig (19%) populated by residents themselves born in Leith. By way of contrast, Edinburgh-born were a weak presence in Leith Colonies and were almost always heavily outnumbered by those who born in the surrounding county area of Midlothian (Edinburghshire) and those adults born across the Firth of Forth in Fife. Given the number of Irish-born in Edinburgh in mid-century their scarcity amongst Colonies residents – 1.4% in Stockbridge; 1.2% in Ferry Road; 1% in Abbeyhill; and 0.7% in Dalry – indicates that the ECBC properties were probably beyond their means and their Old Town networks.

Though it is possible to identify specific geographical patterns, for instance, of the preference of the Inverness-shire and West Lothian-born for Restalrig Colony housing, such numbers were small and require caution. Notwithstanding this, individuals from Shetland and Berwickshire favoured Hawthornbank; Orcadians preferred Ferry Road; and Caithness natives alone accounted for 2.7% of all Colony residents in 1871 and more specifically for 6.0% of Ferry Road Colonists and 7.4% of all Restalrig ones. Glaswegians (2.5%) congregated mainly in Stockbridge and Dalry. One factor that was probably relevant in deciding the area of the city, if not the particular Colony, was the type of transport links. The coastal trade routes to Leith, especially for Fife, Caithness and all East Coast counties were well-established, and the road and rail connections from Lanarkshire favoured west central locations, such as at Dalry.

Arguably the most significant geographical feature of the birthplaces of Colony residents in the 1860s was that only 16.4% were born in Edinburgh and Leith. Put differently, 83.6% of Colonists were not originally from Edinburgh and Leith. This alone suggests a milieu in which incomers to the new Colony housing 'estates' were suddenly confronted with diverse social conventions and regional Scottish dialects, quite apart from those from other parts of Britain. Though Building Associations (see Section 8, Table 8.4) formed new streets it was rare to build entirely new self-contained districts in Edinburgh before the ECBC did so. 'Neighbourhood' assumed a new significance in the urban lexicon from the 1860s.

While the birthplaces of a very large majority of Colonies residents in 1871 indicate that they had roots elsewhere, it is unlikely that the majority migrated and moved immediately into a Colony house. A staged or stepped process was much more likely. Once patterns of work and worship, funds and friends were established sufficiently a nearby 'happy' Colony home was the objective for some. So ECBC housing, while it represented an addition to the overall stock of accommodation, almost certainly was rented or owned by individuals and families who, however briefly, had already become familiar with the city prior to making such a move. In 1861 there were 26,500 residential properties in Edinburgh[7] to which the ECBC added about 900 in the next decade or the equivalent of about 3% of the housing stock of Edinburgh (excluding Leith).

Perhaps a more telling observation (Table 11.1) is that few Edinburgh born moved to Leith Colonies, just as few Leith born moved to Edinburgh ones!

In the second phase of Colony development, the two westernmost settlements North Merchiston and Shaftesbury Park and the Leith Colony of Hermitage Hill shared a common feature – the birthplaces of Colonies residents were dominated (62.4%) by the same six origins as in the first twenty years of ECBC building. The composition had changed radically. Edinburgh-born replaced Midlothian-born as the most common single origin, and whereas Leithers were an endangered species in the 'Flowers' and Shaftesbury homes, they were predictably dominant in the Leith based Hermitage Hill houses, as they had been in the earlier Leith based ones at Hawthornbank and Ferry Road. Lanarkshire born residents were never more numerous than in North Merchiston and Shaftesbury and they, too, like their predecessors at Dalry, seem to confirm a process whereby their arrival from the west predisposed initial settlement in west Edinburgh and subsequently in Colony housing in that same quadrant of the city. Longer distance migrants and the fourth most numerous Colony residents by birthplace were the English born with over 300 residents averaging 8.5% in nine Colonies and over four censuses.

Making a living: ECBC Colonists

Proximity to work was always a major consideration for workers' housing, and continuity at an address was dependent on a relatively regular income. It meant rent arrears or a default on an ECBC mortgage was less likely, and eviction or a flit to a cheaper home unnecessary. Perhaps more than anything else, that fact of regular income conditioned the socio-economic composition of a Colony and, to a certain extent, by employment opportunities within reasonable walking distance of home. The ECBC manager, James Colville, recognised that housing development at Norton Park, Abbeyhill was well positioned for the iron foundries adjoining London Road, and for railway employees on the spaghetti of lines running towards the docks and the St Margaret's railway depot. He commented on the proximity of Norton Park to the Old Town with its various breweries, gasworks, and specialist glass works. In modern parlance it was a landlord's 'no-brainer.' The twin evils of vacancies and defaults were more likely where employment was volatile, seasonal, or casual in the sense of variable hours or days of work.

In addition to birthplaces, therefore, the composition of Edinburgh's Colonies can be seen partly through patterns of work and pay. It seems, initially at least, that consistent with the strike by masons and joiners the emphasis was on housing workers in the building trades. After ten years of construction, these building trades and much smaller numbers of plasterers, painters and plumbers constituted between one-fifth and one-quarter of household heads in the Stockbridge, Hawthornbank, and Dalry Colonies in 1871, and were the largest cohort in the Ferry Road flats. At Abbeyhill and Restalrig the building trades were relegated to third and fourth positions and this reveals how structural and geographical issues in the local economy also played a part in defining the character of Colonies. Whereas 66% of household heads in Stockbridge and 83% in Dalry were from seven major occupational categories, at Norton Park it was just 34%. Conversely, Colony housing at Restalrig was heavily influenced by nearby employment in port-related activities in the 1870s, and this remained the case in all three Leith Colonies during the half century before World War I. At Hermitage Hill the marine-based activities broadened out to involve more professional and supervisory roles rather than the more labour-intensive dock-based

Table 11.3 Colonists' Occupations: Early Developments 1871

Stockbridge (268)	%	Hawthornbank (54)	%	Ferry Road (78)	%
1 building trades	18.7	building trades	22.2	building trades	14.1
2 shopkeeper	10.4	service, personal	16.6	annuitant, retired	11.5
3 clerk	8.6	quarryman	13.0	clerk	6.4
4 professions	8.6	maker/manufacture	9.3	marine	6.4
5 service, personal	7.5	dealer, merchant	9.3	shopkeeper	5.1
6 annuitant, retired	6.3	labourer	7.4	clothing, footwear	5.1
7 clothing, footwear	5.6	professions	3.7	professions	3.8
total – top 7	65.7		81.5		52.6

Norton Park (594)	%	Dalry (127)	%	Restalrig (38)	%
1 printer	9.5	building trades	27.6	railway	23.7
2 clerk	5.4	maker/manufacture	12.6	dealers, merchants	21.1
3 building trades	4.5	clerk	11.8	officials/inspectors	13.2
4 maker/manufacture	4.2	railway	8.7	building trades	10.5
5 shopkeeper	3.9	dealers, merchants	8.7	clerk	10.5
6 clothing, footwear	3.5	service, personal	7.1	annuitant, retired	7.9
7 annuitant, retired	2.9	annuitant, retired	7.0	labourer	5.3
total - top 7	33.9		83.4		92.1

Table 11.4 Colonists' Occupations: Later Developments 1881-1901

1881 North Merchiston (75)	%	1891 Shaftesbury (222)	%	1901 Hermitage Hill (177)	%
1 clerk	21.3	annuitant, retired	17.1	marine, dock	9.5
2 annuitant, retired	16.0	clerk	8.6	dealer, merchant	9.5
3 building trades	13.3	servant (domestic)	7.7	clerk	8.9
4 clothing	8.0	public servant	6.8	professions	8.2
5 furniture maker	8.0	teaching	5.4	annuitant	6.3
6 professions	6.8	agent	5.4	grocer	6.3
7 salesman	4.0	building trades	5.0	clothing	5.7
total - top 7	77.5		55.9		54.4

Source: Census of Edinburgh 1881 – 1901

employment at Restalrig. Neither at Hermitage Hill nor at Norton Park did a single employment group contribute as much as 10% of male household heads and so there was greater social and economic diversity within these Colonies. Indeed Tables 11.3 and 11.4 can be read as follows: the lower the overall percentage of the seven trades identified the greater the extent of occupational diversity amongst household heads and the less likely the Colony was to experience the social, health and related problems of extended bouts of unemployment.

Also revealing in terms of the occupational composition of the Colonies was the presence of pensioners, and others in receipt of 'unearned income.' These were individuals who had sufficient capital, either saved or inherited, to yield a regular income – an annuity. The amount might vary yearly, but only within narrow limits according to adjustments in the rate of interest, or in the dividends issued by companies. Pensions were, therefore, generally more stable than wages and so fixed commitments were manageable by householders and tenants and more attractive to lenders and landlords. This predictably applied also to salaried employees, of whom clerks, professionals, and public servants were examples, and they, too, figured prominently amongst Colony residents. Commerce in the form of dealers and agents, and manufacturers as represented by 'makers' of products were much less common as household heads in the Colonies.

A summary of the occupations of heads of households in eight ECBC Colonies in 1901 shows that the single most frequent occupation was 'annuitant.' There were twice as many such household heads (167) in receipt of interest, dividends, and pensions compared to the next most common sources of income – joiner (84) and clerk (81). When consolidated by employment sector rather than individual occupation, however, the continuing if diminished importance of the building trades remained into the twentieth century (Table 11.5).

When 135 individual occupational descriptions as recorded by census enumerators are consolidated into fifteen manageable employment categories it is possible to capture a more comprehensive overview of the sources of income for 1760 household heads in Colony housing. The relative size of these

Who Lived in the Colonies?

Table 11.5 Occupations of all Colonies Household Heads, 1901

Employment	%	Employment	%
building trades	13.0	personal & domestic services	5.8
transport & communications	11.0	paper & printing	5.7
annuitant	10.9	clerk	5.3
food & drink	8.6	engineering	5.3
commerce & finance	7.8	metalworking	3.1
professions	7.2	unskilled labouring	2.3
clothing & footwear	6.5	music & art	1.0
makers & manufacturers	6.5	total	100.0

Sources: Censuses of Edinburgh, 1871-1901

Note: Total number of household heads (1529) excludes those recording 'no occupation'.

employment sectors in Edinburgh in 1901 is shown in Table 11.5. The mix of occupations conveys something of the nature and balance of work in individual Colonies and reveals subtle yet distinctive differences in the socio-economic and cultural composition of each Colony.

Colonies Women

From the earliest years of Colony housing women were prominent not just as shareholders but also as heads of households. In 1871, almost one in six (15.8%) of all Colony homes had a woman as head of the household; by 1901, this proportion had increased to over one in five (21.5%). Perhaps surprisingly six of the Colonies diverged just a percentage point or two from this overall 21% average (Fig.11.4). Out of step somewhat were the two early Leith developments, Hawthornbank (33%) and Ferry Road, and Dalry which with female heads of household just 7% in 1871 increased dramatically to 28% female headship in 1901.

Householder status was important for women. While their visibility and public engagement became more formalised through organisations such as the Edinburgh National Society for Women's Suffrage (1867) – the first such society in Scotland to campaign for a woman's right to vote – advances in representation were initially obtained through civic bodies and legal decisions. In Edinburgh, the earliest instance of the election of a woman to public office was in the School Board elections of 1873 when Phoebe Blyth and Flora Stevenson stood successfully.

Happy Homes

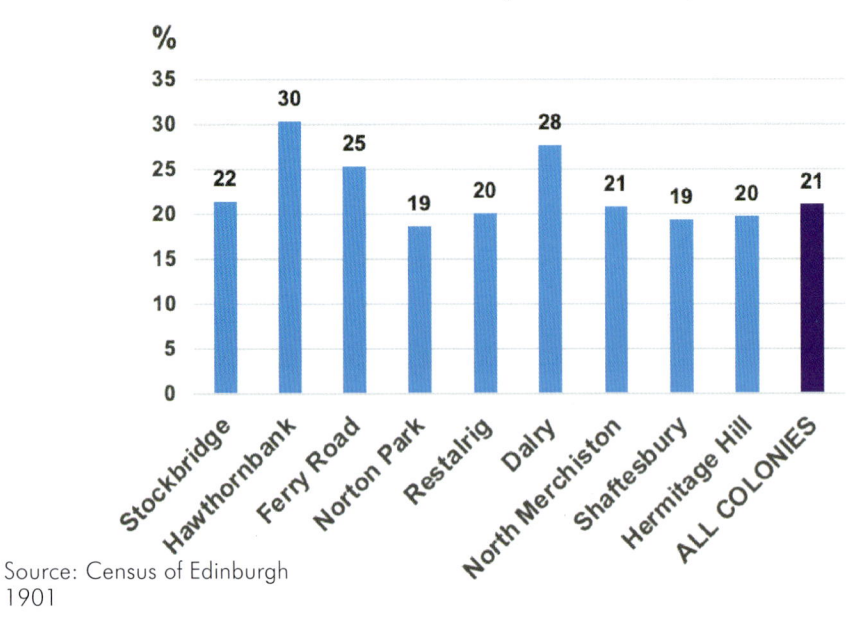

11.4 Female Heads of Colony Households, 1901

Location	%
Stockbridge	22
Hawthornbank	30
Ferry Road	25
Norton Park	19
Restalrig	20
Dalry	28
North Merchiston	21
Shaftesbury	19
Hermitage Hill	20
ALL COLONIES	21

Source: Census of Edinburgh 1901

11.5 Divorce in Edinburgh 1855-1910

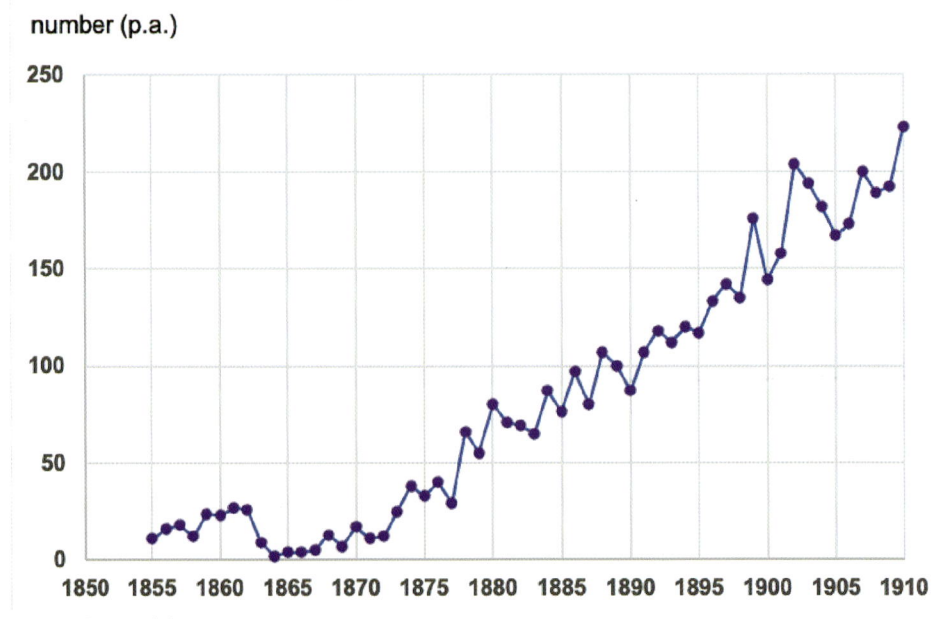

Source: Registrar General for Scotland, Annual Reports, Edinburgh 1855-1911

142

Subsequently, as householders and local taxpayers, the Municipal Elections Amendment (Scotland) Act 1881 enfranchised women ratepayers on the basis that:

> '. . . whenever words occur which import the masculine gender the same shall be held. . . to include females who are not married and married females not living in family with their husbands. . .'[8]

Despite their enfranchisement women were eligible for election as councillors only from 1907.[9]

On 1st November 1861, just a week after Dr James Begg laid the foundation stone for the first ECBC house at Reid Terrace, an important milestone for women's legal status, the Conjugal Rights (Scotland) Act, came into force.[10] Previously, marriage law conferred the right to manage a wife's heritable property on her husband. It was something of a high watermark for male dominance. From 1861, however, any property whether moveable or heritable acquired by a wife after marriage was outside the control of her husband.[11] Also with the divorce rate in Edinburgh climbing quickly in the second half of the nineteenth century (Fig. 11.5) protecting a woman's acquired wealth was an important issue which though not a matter of life and death was one that certainly affected the quality of life and the nature of death. Similarly, since the number of 'never married' and especially middle class never married women also rose appreciably, then the protection of their financial and property assets was never more important.

Women's marital status was highly significant, therefore, for a variety of reasons and the Colonies were a microcosm of their wider experience in Edinburgh and Leith. Of course, the scale was different. Just over 75,000 women were recorded by the enumerator as household heads in Edinburgh and Leith in the four censuses between 1871 and 1901, and just under 1,000 of them lived in ECBC-built Colony homes where widows accounted for 57% of female household heads (Table 11.6). This was exactly the same percentage as in Edinburgh generally, and just 1% above the corresponding figure for widows in Leith (56%). Married (18%) and unmarried (25%) status accounted for the other 43% of female heads of ECBC households – the exact reverse of the percentages in Leith housing. Annuities were the most common single source of income (35%) amongst unmarried heads of households, while housekeepers, dressmakers, and servants collectively accounted for 40%.

The relationship between marital status and household head status was a complex one. With one exception (widows) the average age of ECBC heads of households, both male and female, was about 2-3 years younger than in the city overall in 1871. The new Colony housing developments were seen as desirable and affordable to occupational groups which included significant numbers of clerks, annuitants, merchants and building trades workers (Tables 11.3). Indeed, it was both a measure of the purchasing power of these occupations that they could form independent households a couple of years earlier that the city-wide average and a reflection of how older Edinburgh residents could not afford or contemplate a move to an ECBC home.

By 1901 the relationship between ECBC household heads and marital status was rather different. The city-wide averages had altered no more than a point or two, but the ECBC household heads were generally older – and specifically were older in four of the six categories (Table 11.7). Conceivably the later, larger and more elaborate Colony houses were just more expensive and so that purchases or rentals were deferred by a couple of years. Certainly the occupational composition of the ECBC Colonies altered to become more diverse in the 1880s and 1890s (Table 11.5).

To these complicated social dynamics and improving real wages in the last third of the nineteenth century three other factors had a bearing on ECBC Colony housing. Firstly, a decline in birth rates contributed to a reduction in family size; secondly, infant mortality in Edinburgh declined from about 140/1000 to 110/1000 between the 1890 and 1910; and thirdly, after 1885 the newly formed Scottish Education Department sought to extend post-elementary schooling and, as a result, children became a financial burden to many families rather than economic assets contributing to the family budget.

There is evidence that the Colonies experienced at least some of the effects of wider social trends. Indeed, it would be strange

Who Lived in the Colonies?

Table 11.6 Average Age of Household Heads 1871

marital status	ECBC females	Edinburgh females	ECBC males	Edinburgh males
single	44.1	46.9	27.1	31.0
married	39.7	41.2	38.9	41.9
widowed	57.6	56.7	51.0	56.2

Table 11.7 Average Age of Household Heads 1901

marital status	ECBC females	Edinburgh females	ECBC males	Edinburgh males
single	46.8	45.0	31.5	32.6
married	31.5	42.6	43.6	42.6
widowed	60.1	57.6	58.4	57.7

Source: Census of Scotland, Edinburgh 1871 and 1901.

Note: Lodgers accounted for 4% of residents in both colony housing and in the housing stock of Edinburgh and Leith.

if they were exempt. Except for Ferry Road, all Colonies experienced a reduction in the average household size from the 1880s (Table 11.8) and were in the range 4-5 persons per household. For some (Stockbridge, Hawthornbank and Ferry Road) this was achieved partly through a reduction in the frequency of larger households – those with five or more persons. In others (Norton Park, Restalrig and Dalry) though the number of five plus households increased, this was offset sufficiently by the frequency of smaller households to record a decline in average household size in these Colonies.

Source: Census of Edinburgh, 1871-1901

Table 11.8 Average Household Size by Colony 1871-1901

colony	1871	1881	1891	1901	overall
Stockbridge	4.1	4.8	4.2	4.3	4.4
Hawthornbank	4.7	5.3	4.5	3.9	4.5
Ferry Road	3.8	4.1	3.9	3.7	3.8
Norton Park	4.0	4.9	4.4	4.0	4.3
Restalrig Park	4.9	4.7	4.7	4.3	4.6
Dalry	4.9	5.1	4.5	4.0	4.6
West Barnton Terr		4.0	4.1	4.1	4.1
North Merchiston		4.6	4.6	4.4	4.5
Shaftesbury Park				4.1	4.1
Hermitage Hill				4.4	4.4
all	4.3	4.8	4.4	4.2	4.4

The Finale

To claim that the socio-economic characteristics of Colony housing had much, if anything, to do with the ECBC itself would be misleading. Indeed, the ECBC business model required as rapid a turnover as possible. Whether by an outright sale to an individual purchaser, or to a property company to add to their rental portfolio, or as part of a mortgage arrangement with the owner buying a house through regular payments either to the ECBC or another lender, the commercial priority was to shed the Colony houses as soon as possible in order to release capital to buy more land and build more houses.

The business model was applied from the very start. The original Colony houses, Reid Terrace, were mostly sold to private individuals, but in the adjoining terrace, Hugh Miller Place, there was an immediate sale of several properties to a single buyer who then rented the individual properties. The ECBC, therefore, provided opportunities for landlordism. However, had the ECBC itself held on to the properties it had built then this would have committed capital for at least 14 years if the standard repayment model applied, as explained by Begg's 'Snuff and Smoke' example. There were also ongoing land charges, collection costs and local taxes, each of which ate into the gross rental revenue of a property.

Half a century later the same model was still in use. However, unlike the Stockbridge site, the Shaftesbury houses were assessed in 1911 for local taxation purposes at £17-23 p.a. and Cornhill and Ryehill houses (Fig.11.7) at Hermitage Hill were at rentals of £20-23 p.a.[11] This was equivalent to about 40% of most manual workers annual wages – generally considered to be 'Round about a Pound a Week' before 1914.[12] For them a Hermitage Hill home was out of the question. Typically, therefore, it was a 53-year old mercantile clerk, John Knox, who could afford to live in a three-room house at 25 Cornhill Terrace with his two daughters. It was Robert Rutherford, aged 33, a marine engineer with a wife and three sons, who could afford 7 Ryehill Terrace. ECBC properties at 1-7 and 9-13 East Restalrig Terrace were homes affordable by a headmaster, two teachers, a spirit merchant, master stevedore, saw miller, draper, two commercial agents, a funeral undertaker, and a manager.

At Hermitage Hill seven out of every ten completed properties were promptly sold to individual owners. Artisans of the 'labour aristocracy' at Stockbridge were gradually replaced by a 'petit bourgeoisie' of shopkeepers, clerks, and eventually also by professionally qualified teachers and engineers so that by the twentieth century building trades workers were increasingly priced out of the ECBC properties (Table 11.4)

The undoubted success of building and sales at Hermitage Hill obscured some of the weaknesses that emerged in the ECBC. As early as the 1880s the ECBC changed fundamentally from a building company to a letting company with housebuilding interests. An analysis of the balance sheets of the ECBC in its first fifty years provides convincing confirmation of this transition which can even be traced to the hiatus over land acquisitions in the mid-1870s. The value of houses sold and unsold, broadly speaking, tracked one another until the early 1880s (Fig.11.7). Thereafter, the divergence was pronounced. Unsold houses (black) continued to rise, tracked by lettings (grey) as the ECBC increasingly became a landlord. Even the housebuilding boom of the late-1890s ultimately added to unsold stock after a brief reprieve between 1898 and 1902. In this light the demise of the ECBC in the twentieth century and specifically in the 1920s and 1930s was not entirely surprising.

Though the ECBC management had difficulty in securing suitable sites initially some landowners such as the trustees of James Walker (Dalry), Lady Menzies (Abbeyhill) and the Merchant Company (North Merchiston; Shaftesbury Park) saw the benefit to themselves of relinquishing plots. The ECBC established itself literally in a niche market – a niche that was the development of land that was indeed marginal, squeezed as it was between railway lines, industrial sites, and arterial roads. In many respects this was the ECBC norm and in corresponded with what might be termed conventional building firms such as those of James Steel (Drumdryan) or W.&D. MacGregor (Glengyle) or even Building Associations who acquired modest plots, completed them, and moved on.

The ECBC's purchase of the Baird's Saughton estate was of a greenfield site (Balgreen). Its extent and location were unfamiliar

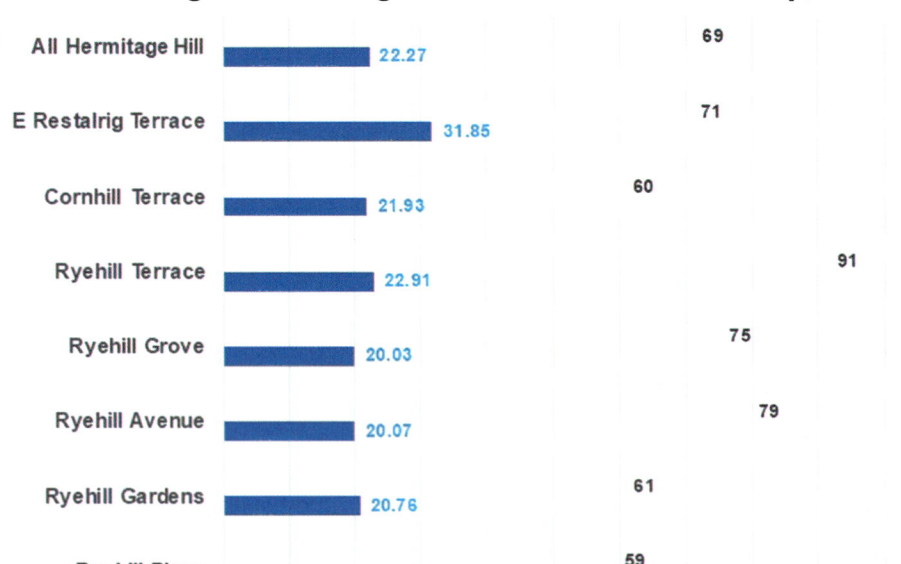

11.6 Hermitage Hill: Average Rents and Home Ownership, 1911

Location	Average Assessed Rent (£)	Owner Occupied (%)
All Hermitage Hill	22.27	69
E Restalrig Terrace	31.85	71
Cornhill Terrace	21.93	60
Ryehill Terrace	22.91	91
Ryehill Grove	20.03	75
Ryehill Avenue	20.07	79
Ryehill Gardens	20.76	61
Ryehill Place	20.22	59

Source: NRS Valuation Rolls, VR55 130, Leith 1910-11

to the management. It was the largest plot acquired by the ECBC and obtained at a time when the building cycle entered its deepest recession for over a generation, and when the Company was already heavily committed to Hermitage Hill. Whereas before 1905 the ECBC obtained land, built houses, and sold homes for rental to owner occupiers, landlords and property companies, from that date the Company increasingly missed out the building step. It sold land to development and building companies directly. There was little or no pretence that the ECBC was building 'Happy Homes for Working Men' and there were no indications as to 'How to Get Them'. Furthermore, from its foundation the distribution of an average annual dividend (1862-1914) of 11.9% deprived the ECBC of a reservoir of developmental capital and a financial cushion when it was in difficulty and most needed. This affirmation of financial probity was a guiding principle of ECBC decision-making. The conservatism of management so typical of many industrial sectors in Britain in the last quarter of the nineteenth century came back to haunt the Company.

11.8 ECBC Sales and Lettings 1865-1914

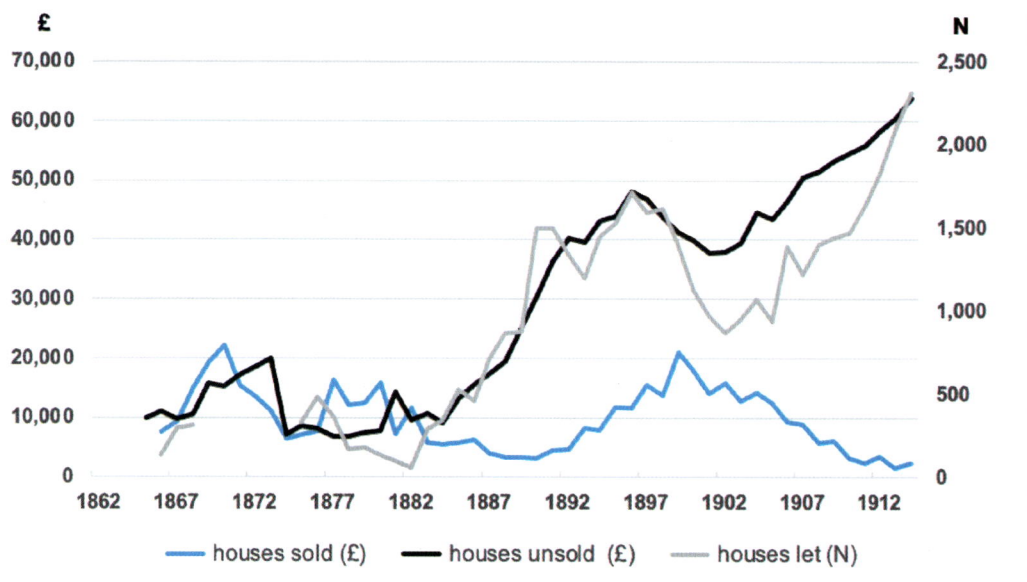

11.8 ECBC Sales and Lettings 1865-1914
Source: NRS ECBC

In mitigation, the ECBC was not to know the length and depth of depression, and by selling plots to other developers it did not incur full land charges. Nor in 1919 could it have anticipated the 'Homes Fit For Heroes' election campaign, nor the subsequent and more extensive subsidies to private builders under the Housing Acts of 1923 and 1924. While land acquisitions had been a particular difficulty before 1900, weakness in the land market was not the problem in the inter-war years – it was housebuilding. This was exacerbated by a conservative approach of the ECBC's pre-war style of terraced house which was at odds with the new post-war designs, methods, and materials.

Happy Homes

Shaftesbury Park Colonies

PHOTO: John Reiach

12. Legacies

NOTHING should detract from the remarkable and durable achievements of the Edinburgh Cooperative Building Company Limited. As one of the earliest Limited Liability Companies in Edinburgh and, indeed, in Scotland, a steering group of stonemasons shaped the Articles of Association and the governance of the ECBC. The founders addressed the logistical challenges of managing multiple building sites simultaneously and introduced artisans to the concept of mortgages as a means towards house purchase and ownership. For these reasons alone, the ECBC was a remarkable local organisation. It was inspirational, too, in the foundation of similar housing developments in Burntisland, Leven, Musselburgh and Rutherglen, as well as locally amongst private developers at Industrial Road, Leith and in Lower London Road and Ardmillan Place (Fig. 12.1).

It is no exaggeration to claim that from the 1860s the ECBC enhanced political participation through house ownership. Residential property worth £10 per annum rental or more entitled both men and women to vote and stand for office. This was a development almost unimaginable a generation previously. Continuity at an address conveyed not just voting rights but, importantly, was also associated with stability – in the neighbourhood, and in religious organisations, and in civil society generally. Fixed capital in the form of a Colony house also came with social capital. In practical terms this meant continuity at school for children, and an improved life expectancy. The lesser the likelihood of illness, the greater the continuity of employment, and the more remote the implosion of the family budget, eviction, and a downward spiral into poverty.

In its first ten years the Edinburgh Cooperative Building Company Limited built over 900 homes worth £14.9 million in 2020 prices; by 1914 the company had built over 2,800 properties and housed 12,650 people in 'Happy Homes' built at a cost equivalent to £93

12.1 Distinctive external stair access
in (l to r) Fisherrow, Burntisland, Methil, and Rutherglen

million nowadays. It was a level of residential construction sufficient in 1914 to house an entire medium-sized Scottish town. As for standards of construction the earliest Colony houses, now 160 years old, have proved exceptionally durable. None has been demolished as unsound though a few have made way for adaptations as shops. Solidity of construction might suggest outmoded design and from the 1920s the ECBC management was indeed unresponsive to changing market conditions and subsidy arrangements. Nevertheless, the pre-1914 ECBC houses continue in 2022 to have an enduring appeal and an affectionate and recognisable place in Edinburgh folk memory, sufficient for private sector housebuilders to provide twentieth century copies at Leith Fort. At Cammo Meadows, by contrast, the developer states in their publicity that 'the Colony home is an iconic element of Edinburgh's celebrated architecture'[1] and thereby attempts to leech historical validity for contemporary houses that bear little resemblance to homes that Begg, Colville and thousands of Colonies residents would recognise.

Not only were ECBC homes scattered across the 'colonial' outskirts of the pre-1914 city as it then was, but their locations also contributed to a centrifugal effect on the population distribution in the city. The ECBC houses demonstrated an important principle: environmental health 'Improvements' need not necessarily require the demolition of tenements and the destruction of city centre communities. Suburbanisation, often associated with middle class flight from insanitary central districts, was to some extent anticipated in the 1860s by the cooperative zeal displayed by Edinburgh building tradesmen and the ECBC.

James Colville's experience as a mason and his thirty-year stint as ECBC manager was itself an assurance of quality and continuity. Reputationally there was concern for, and pride in, the quality of the ECBC product. Colville was the enforcer. However, rigour was not just about the structural stonework or the quality of the skilled craftsmanship. It was about amenities and standards too. Thought was given to the nature and location of the range, and to the cistern and piped running water to the kitchen sink and W.C. Dormer windows were introduced to improve light; storage space in the attic was used imaginatively; and an outdoor store accommodated coal and gardening tools. These were the hallmarks of ECBC housing as much as the distinctive external staircase or barleycorn iron railings and clothes poles. Crucially, too, ground floor living accounted for 50% of ECBC homes – a radical departure from conventional tenements where it was at best 20%. Each feature marked a fundamental departure from city centre tenement living and, though some of these amenities were established elements in villa houses elsewhere in the city, never on such a scale were these amenities previously both available and affordable to skilled craftsmen.

Invariably social interactions and the 'lived experience' generally were fundamentally different in ECBC designed homes. The ECBC set a standard in the 1860s. Convenience and comfort were considerations beyond villadom. Varied floor plans in Colony houses proved attractive to different family sizes, budgets, and life-cycle stages. This was a perceptive distinction founded on a detailed knowledge of working-class budgets and the significance of modest differentials in rents.

Another legacy, a durable sense of community, developed by virtue of the parallel terraces and, most importantly, self-contained Colony streets. Through traffic was, and still is, not possible in eight of the eleven ECBC Colonies.[2] This single element was a master stroke. It needed no master plan. ECBC Colony lay-outs provided a built environment in which street games and neighbourly chat were facilitated by the layout of parallel terraces with a high proportion of ground floor entrances. Social interactions were inescapable and encouraged a sense of community without endangering privacy. Parallel lines of terraced housing and the barriers to traffic routes provided a clear demarcation of a Colony area, visible in aerial photography, and even from space. This sense of identity for each Colony emerged both from its confined extent and its distinctiveness from the ubiquitous four-storey tenement housing which subsequently proliferated around the Colonies in the last quarter of the nineteenth century. These were some of the elements that explain why Colony housing in Edinburgh differed fundamentally from English terraced housing.

Cooperation, community, and co-ownership of shared spaces were the fundamental principles enshrined in the ECBC's Memorandum of Association. These were values consistent with those of the Cooperative Movement. However, to achieve as much as it did, the ECBC was forced to compromise. For all its determination to focus on working men and house-ownership, the reality of the market was rather different and the ECBC readily agreed to sales and rental agreements with teachers, shopkeepers, and clerks as well as the annuitants living on the proceeds of financial investments. As a result, the building trades and manual workers declined as a proportion of those housed in ECBC properties both as owners and as tenants (see Fig.8.3).

Increasingly, individuals with 'unearned income' owned Colony houses. By 1914 a third of all Colony homes were owned by someone with two or more houses. Ownership and occupancy became increasingly detached. Rather than a honeycomb of private ownership as initially conceived by the founders and as described by James Begg, clusters of properties owned by relatively wealthy individuals and property companies such as the Suburban Feuing Company and the Scottish Metropolitan Property Company were common. Trusts owned 13% of all shares. Even before the first Colony houses had been completed in Stockbridge it was recognised that they were a sound investment for at least three reasons. ECBC houses were soundly constructed; they incurred lower maintenance costs as a result; and were probably offered at prices below market value so that they would be affordable to workmen.[3] The result overall was that significant numbers of Colony houses were owned by absentee landlords who employed one of the innumerable letting agents in the city to manage their property. As a result, the ECBC reproduced the landlord-tenant relations of the private rental market with their inherent tensions based around the different roles and interests of factors, agents, collectors and, occasionally, bailiffs.

There is little reason to think that investors, or their agents, had much interest in cooperative ideals. More likely, through the Edinburgh Stock Exchange, they sought to obtain ECBC shares which yielded a very attractive annual average dividend of 11.9% in the period 1861 to 1914.[4] So from the outset there was a considerable shift in the composition of ECBC shareholders. More than half the shares initially taken up by building tradesmen were sold and then bought by three broad groups: clerks, merchants or dealers, and rentiers. As a direct consequence of this shift in share ownership there was a corresponding shift in the residential distribution of shareholders. Initial clusters in 1861 in St Leonard's, Causewayside, Tollcross, and the Old Town were replaced by 1914 by clusters in the northern New Town around Broughton and Bellevue, Stockbridge and Silvermills, and scattered widely in Marchmont, Merchiston and Morningside.

South Leith shareholders' addresses were replaced by ones in North Leith.

Absentees increasingly acquired house-ownership in the Colonies. Within four years of its foundation, the ECBC share register recorded addresses in Glasgow and London, as well as in Wick, Forfar, Penicuik and small-town Scotland more generally.[5] From Kirkcudbright to Caithness investors placed their modest private savings and trust funds in the ECBC and so facilitated the construction of housing in Edinburgh and Leith. By 1914, ECBC shareholders resident in Edinburgh and Leith still accounted for 70% of all shareholders, though a mere 6.5% actually lived in a Colony house.[6]

Perhaps of greater significance was the skewed nature of ECBC shareholding: 44% of shareholders controlled only 10% of shares. Conversely, just 56 individuals or 12% of shareholders held 50% of ECBC shares. Of the largest twenty shareholders, fourteen were either trusts or women or non-resident in Edinburgh, and since their shares were generally managed by an agent it is not surprising that shareholder input to Company policy was so reduced that executive power became progressively influenced more by dividends and financial results than by building 'Happy Homes' for working men and their families. In this respect the geographical diffusion of ownership both at some distance from Edinburgh and detached from building industry operatives placed the ECBC increasingly in the mainstream of financial transactions rather than, as the founders intended, in the hands of labour.

At a personal level there was emotional baggage in holding ECBC shares. Annie Mein used the dividends from her late husband's ECBC investment to pay the bills on 40 Ivy Terrace, the house they bought together from the Company not long after it was built. The son and daughter of two ECBC Directors, David Rintoul and Daniel Kemp, retained shares inherited from their founding fathers. Sometimes members of the same household acquired shares in the ECBC, as with Andrew Drummond, a commercial clerk, and his three unmarried sisters, Isabella, Williamina, and Alice who accumulated 113 shares amongst them to fund their shared home at 17 Gardner's Crescent. In these and other respects the ECBC's homes were not unlike those in the rental market generally. For the Drummond sisters and many others their ECBC shares provided a financial cushion and ECBC dividend payments provided an income stream. This was attractive to women whether married, widowed or unmarried. In fact, women owned two in every five shares (41%), half of which were held by unmarried women.

Consequently, the rhythm of ECBC construction was consistent with, rather than independent of, the fluctuations in the building industry. The ECBC management was drawn into discussions concerning profits, dividends, share-owning, and landownership. There was an underlying tension between the principles of cooperation and consultation inherent in a mutual society and the imperatives of the market which required prompt decision-making by a few individuals. Consequently, the initial focus enshrined in official documents and public pronouncements about 'homes for working men' were increasingly interpreted not to be targeted just at artisans but at a 'petit bourgeoisie' of clerks and pensioners, shopkeepers and public officials.

Any independent observer, or indeed the ECBC founders themselves, if presented with a stocktaking of Company activities would agree that the survival of a firm for half a century in the building industry was indeed a major achievement. No less so was the construction of over 2565 homes capable of housing 12500 individuals on eleven discrete housing estates. The distribution of dividends in each of fifty years – never less than 7.5% and often 10% – was a highly successful strategy for ECBC investors, many of whom were women who gained equal voting rights and a public voice in the governance of the ECBC at the quarterly and annual meetings of the Company. Perhaps the enduring testimonial should be that 160 years later Edinburgh Colony houses built by the ECBC are held in high regard and warm affection amongst Edinburgh folks. That they are still much sought after is perhaps the most fitting testimonial.

Happy Homes

Appendix 1

List of Streets, Edinburgh Cooperative Building Company Ltd.

Stockbridge (1861)
Reid Terrace
Hugh Miller Place
Rintoul Place
Colville Place
Collins Place
Bell Place
Kemp Place
Glenogle Place
Glenogle Terrace
Glenogle House
Avondale Place
Teviotdale Place
Balmoral Place
Dunrobin Place
Bridge Place

Leith (1863)
Hawthornbank Place
Hawthornbank Terrace

Ferry Road (1864)
Henderson Place/Ferry Road
Trafalgar Street

Norton Park (1866) or Maryfield or Abbeyhill
Maryfield Place
Alva Place
Lady Menzies Place
Regent Place
Waverley Place

Carlyle Place
Pitlochry Place
Salmond Place
Earlston Place

Dalry (1866)
Cobden Terrace
Bright Terrace
McLaren Terrace
Douglas Terrace
Argyll Terrace
Atholl Terrace
Lewis Terrace
Walker Terrace
Breadalbane Terrace
Breadalbane Cottages

Restalrig Park (1866)
Woodville Terrace
Woodbine Terrace
Thornville Terrace
Ashville Terrace
Beechwood Terrace
Elmwood Terrace
Oakville Terrace

West Barnton Terrace (1877)

North Merchiston (1877)
Daisy Terrace
Lily Terrace
Ivy Terrace

Happy Homes

Primrose Terrace
Myrtle Terrace
Laurel Terrace
Violet Terrace

Shaftesbury (1883)
Hazelbank Terrace
Hollybank Terrace
Almondbank Terrace
Briarbank Terrace
Alderbank Terrace
Alderbank Place
Alderbank Gardens

Hermitage Hill (1890)
East Restalrig Terrace
Restalrig Terrace
Cornhill Terrace
Ryehill Terrace
Ryehill Gardens
Ryehill Grove
Ryehill Avenue
Ryehill Place
Summerfield Place

Balgreen (1902)
Balgreen Road
Balgreen Avenue
Glendevon Place
Saughtonhall Drive
Saughton Crescent

Appendix 2

Edinburgh Cooperative Building Company Residents and Households										
colony	1871 persons	1871 house-holds	1881 persons	1881 house-holds	1891 persons	1891 house-holds	1901 persons	1901 house-holds	properties no.	house-hold size (av.)
1 Stockbridge	1184	291	1682	350	1644	388	1614	372	377	4.3
2 Hawthornbank	231	49	206	39	206	46	178	46	44	3.9
3 Ferry Road	228	60	232	57	247	64	201	60	60	3.3
4 Norton Park	731	181	1579	325	1676	383	2431	566	566	4.3
5 Restalrig Park	186	38	773	164	891	190	833	194	208	4.3
6 Dalry	558	133	620	123	615	124	681	130	140	5.2
7 N. Merchiston	–	–	354	77	705	154	771	177	157	4.4
9 Shaftesbury Pk	–	–	–	–	536	131	932	227	330	4.1
10 Hermitage Hill	–	–	–	–	–	–	751	172	361	4.4
11 Balgreen	–	–	–	–	–	–	834	191	191	4.4
8 Barnton Terrace	–	–							9	
	3118	752	5446	1135	6520	1480	9226	2135	2443	
							9687	2242	2565	

Note: the number of Colony households and properties do not correspond due to vacancies, absences on census night, and buildings in progress.

Sources: Census of Edinburgh, 1871-1901; Valuation Rolls, Edinburgh and Leith, 1861, 1913; NRS, GD 327/488 Edinburgh Cooperative Building Company 1862-1917

Household Heads: Persistence at the Same Address 1871 and 1891

	same head	number of houses	%
Douglas Terrace	6	15	40.0
Hawthornbank Place	8	21	38.1
Hawthornbank Terrace	8	21	38.1
Cobden Terrace	4	16	25.0
Woodbine Terrace	7	28	25.0
Maryfield	10	46	21.7
Atholl Terrace	3	16	18.8
Rintoul Place	6	32	18.8
Colville Place	5	30	16.7
Lady Menzies Place	8	49	16.3
Kemp Place	5	33	15.2
Reid Terrace	7	40	17.5
Bright Terrace	2	14	14.3
Argyll Terrace	2	16	12.5
Glenogle Terrace	1	8	12.5
Bell Place	4	33	12.1
McLaren Terrace	1	9	11.1
Trafalgar Street	3	29	10.3
Alva Place	5	49	10.2
Woodville Terrace	1	10	10.0
Lewis Terrace	1	11	9.1
Breadalbane Terrace	1	19	5.3
Collins Place	1	29	3.4
Hugh Miller Place	1	32	3.1
Henderson Place	1	40	2.5
	101	**646**	**15.6**

Appendix 3

ECBC Houses still owned by E. B. Contractors in 1943

Lily Terrace, 7, 10

Ashley Terrace 31, 35,

Hazelbank Terrace 6, 15, 25, 29, 35, 36, 38, 42, 46, 51, 52, 58, 59, 65, 67

Hollybank Terrace 20, 23, 31

Almondbank Terrace 28

Briarbank Terrace 28

Alderbank Terrace 6

Balgreen Road 76, 78, 80

Glendevon Place 13, 44, 56

East Restalrig Terrace 28, 46, 50, 56, 63, 65

Restalrig Road 38, 50, 54, 68, 82

Cornhill Terrace 38, 86

Ryehill Place 2, 4

Ryehill Gardens 37

Ryehill Avenue 2

Castle Street 32

Book value £26,000

Source: NRS GD327/496/3 Houses Rented 1943

Appendix 4

The Edinburgh Cooperative Building Company (ECBC): 'founders' and figureheads

Reverend Dr James Begg (1808-1883) was one of the first Ministers of the Free Church of Scotland, formed in 1843, and although a traditionalist within the Church was notable for his achievements as a social reformer and campaigner for improvements in the housing conditions of working people. Begg developed an eight-point charter in 1850 and in the same year published his 'Social Reform: how every man may become his own landlord' in which he set out how to provide more employment for the poor. A second publication that year focused on Edinburgh improvements. Begg was a prolific letter writer to *The Scotsman* on matters relating to housing conditions and authored *Happy Homes for Working Men, and How to Get Them* (1866) which also provided a background to the Edinburgh Cooperative Building Company. James Begg and his young wife, Maria, were both from New Monkland, Lanarkshire and had six children – three boys and three girls – who in 1861 were aged between 3 and 17. The family lived first at the Newington Free Church Manse in Cumin Place, and then at 50 George Square.

Rev Dr Wiliam Garden Blaikie (1820-99) was an Aberdonian, a theological student of Thomas Chalmers, and one of the 474 secessionists in the Disruption in 1843. Blaikie was 'translated' from Turriff to Pilrig Free Church as minister in 1844. He was a prolific pamphleteer for the Free Church cause and authored over 60 publications including *Six Lectures addressed to the Working Classes on the Improvement of their Temporal Condition* (3rd edn., 1849). His *Better Days for Working People* sold 60,000 copies. Blaikie's Free Kirk credentials were impressive – he was Moderator in 1892 and Editor of the Free Church Magazine. Blaikie was networked through his kirk elders, with Francis Brown Douglas (later Lord Provost) and David Cousin (later City Architect) who, with John Lessels, was heavily involved in the reconstruction of the Old Town and the Edinburgh Improvement Trust from 1867.

Reverend Dr Thomas Chalmers (1780-1847) was born in Anstruther, studied at the Universities of St Andrews and Edinburgh, ordained minister of Kilmany parish church, Fife in 1803, then at Tron Church Glasgow. Known for his evangelical preaching and vocal in efforts to improve the social condition of parishioners in Glasgow. Advocated a church building programme to address the education and pastoral needs of the rapidly expanding city. Appointed as professor of moral philosophy at St Andrews (1823) and then as professor of theology at Edinburgh University (1828). He lived at 3 Forres Street in the New Town and spent some time touring Scottish parishes in his role as chair of the Church Extension Committee. Chalmers opposed church appointments by external bodies and argued that the parish should appoint ministers. This led in 1843 to the Disruption, the foundation of the Free Church of Scotland, and an intensive church building programme. Noted for his passionate oratory, and prolific writings. Died Morningside, Edinburgh 1847; survived by his wife and six daughters. Chalmers' burial was the first in Grange Cemetery, Edinburgh.

James Colville (1822-1892) and his wife, Elizabeth, were both born in Dunfermline, and arrived in Edinburgh in the 1840s where they lived with their four daughters and a son, Edinburgh-born children, in a congested New Town block in Clyde Street. Colville then moved the family to Scotland Street, close to an area of north Edinburgh extending from Henderson Row to Stockbridge and beyond to Bedford Street. It was an area served by the Northern Cooperative Association, a splinter from the St Cuthbert's Cooperative, and was home to many of the striking masons in 1861 and subsequent signatories of the Edinburgh Cooperative Building Company's Memorandum of Association. An ex-President of the Masons' Union, and one of the founding stonemasons of the ECBC, Colville served as the Company's full-time Manager from its formation in 1861 until his retirement aged 67 in 1889 with an honorarium of £100. During this time Colville and his family lived in the Stockbridge Colonies first at 32 Bell Place and then at 16 Kemp Place close to where the Company's building yard and site office were located for many years. Colville was made a Justice of the Peace in 1886, thus becoming the first 'workman magistrate' in the city.

Happy Homes

Sir James Gowans (1821-1890) Born at Blackness near Bo'ness on the Firth of Forth, Gowans followed his father's occupation as a builder. He gained experience studying and working with the highly regarded architect David Bryce, and then worked independently from 1846. Gowans built, and lived in, Rosebank Cottages, blocks of model houses near Fountainbridge which with its parallel terraces and balcony access pre-dated a design similar to that of the Colonies. He built tenements at Cornwall Street and Castle Terrace where he also lived. Gowans owned and operated several quarries, undertook railway building contracts, and constructed tram lines between Edinburgh and Leith. He became Lord Dean of Guild – chairman of the body responsible for approving building plans in the city – and was also chairman of the Committee that supervised the Edinburgh International Exhibition on the Meadows in 1886, for which he was knighted. He was buried in Grange Cemetery.

Daniel Kemp (1810-1886) was born in Edinburgh began his working life as a confectioner, but eventually became connected with the management of the poor while in Wrexham between c.1836 and 1856. This led to the appointment of Governor of the City of Edinburgh Poorhouse, from 1856 until till his death in 1886. Like his younger brother (David) he took a deep interest in the Baptist church and was for many years a pastor (unpaid) of the Bristo Place Baptist Chapel, Edinburgh. The Kemp family had a long and close association with the ECBC from its beginning in 1861. Daniel Kemp, after whom Kemp Place is named, became one of the first directors of the ECBC. Of his two sons, Daniel William, married Helen Primrose Bell in 1869, and was an ECBC director for most of his life, and became a JP and Liberal Councillor for Leith West for some years. David was the ECBC treasurer for 24 years. His grandson Charles also became an ECBC director.

Hugh Miller (1802-1856) Although he had committed suicide before the ECBC was formed, Miller was nevertheless honoured by the Company (Hugh Miller Place) for his influence in raising public awareness of the need for more and better housing for working people. Born and educated in Cromarty, Miller was also a stonemason, geologist, writer, political activist, and editor of the Free Church newspaper *The Witness*. He lived at 2 Stuart Street in 1851 with his Inverness-born wife, Lydia Fraser (married 1837) a children's author, and their two daughters (Harriet and Elizabeth, and two sons William and Hugh. Miller was buried in Grange cemetery, Edinburgh.

Sir Hugh Gilzean Reid (1836-1911), whose name was given to the first terrace built by the ECBC, is often described as its 'founder' since it was he who assisted a group of stonemasons to set up the Company in 1861. Reid was a lifelong campaigner for the cooperative movement and for the improvement of working people's living and working conditions. He described and promoted the work of the ECBC in his book *Housing the People: An Example in Cooperation*. Born in Cruden Bay, Aberdeenshire, Reid described himself as a newspaper writer and lived in Lothian Street when he came to work in Edinburgh. By profession a journalist, Reid edited, founded, and owned various newspapers in Scotland and England, including the *Edinburgh Weekly News* and openly supported and encouraged working men's organisations. He moved to Middlesbrough as a newspaper editor and served as a Liberal MP for Aston (1885-86), near Birmingham, in Gladstone's Government and was knighted in 1893.

Signatories to the Memorandum of Association

What is striking about the initial page of subscribers to the Edinburgh Cooperative Building Company Ltd., is that though all of them were masons none was born in Edinburgh. **David Rintoul** (£5) was the first and **James Collins** (£1) the third of the subscribers to the ECBC on, appropriately, Independence Day 4 July 1861. Rintoul was from Perth, as was his wife, Helen, and after living initially in North Haugh Street, Stockbridge they raised their four boys and two girls for over thirty years at the family home, 24 Reid Terrace. Collins was a 'stonecutter' (mason) from Coupar Angus, Perthshire and lived at 18 Bedford Street where he rented a flat from the Rev. J. Dow for £6 per year. Stockbridge terraces were named after Rintoul, Collins, and David Bell a loyal ECBC supporter. Bell was skilled joiner from Lauder in Berwickshire, who lived first at India Place, Stockbridge, then at 27 Rintoul Place, and Bell served on the ECBC committee until he resigned to start up his own building business in 1869. The fourth subscriber was **William Mill** (b.1838) (£5), a 23-year-old unmarried mason from Monikie, Forfarshire, living in Earl Grey Street. **George Mill** (b.1843) a joiner, also from Monikie, Forfarshire was 18 at the time, and ten years later George and his wife Jessie (from St Andrews) were living in the model dwellings at 29 Patriot Hall, Hamilton Place and so had strong credentials in relation to the model housing, the ECBC and the Cooperative movement generally. As the family expanded (two boys and two girls born) the Mill family moved a few hundred yards to larger accommodation at 19 and then 17 Henderson Row, and in 1889 George was appointed during a rather lean spell of housebuilding to the General Manager's post following the retirement of James Colville in 1890. The family moved to 26 Eyre Place in the 1890s. **James Earshman** (£1) Blackford Cottage, Canaan Lane from Lochmaben, Dumfriesshire was a 26-year-old mason and was the sixth signatory to the ECBC's Memorandum of Association in 1861. He and his wife, Isabella, from East Lothian, had an 8-month-old son James jr., who became a stonemason 20 years later. At the time of signing the family shared their cottage with James' brother John, another stonemason. The family subsequently moved to 16 Beaumont Place and then to 64 Buccleuch Place. **John Ogilvie** (£5) from Cameron Bridge, Fife was the second named subscriber to the ECBC and lived in Holyrood Street, in Edinburgh's Canongate. **Thomas Morgan**, (£3) the fifth signatory in 1861 came originally from Halkirk in Caithness and rented a flat at North Haugh Street, almost on the Stock Bridge itself, for £6 per year, and moved to 23 Downie Place, Tollcross with his wife a few years later. **John W. Syme** (£5) was the seventh and final signature on the initial page of the ECBC Memorandum of Association. Syme was a 32-year old mason from Cupar, Fife who with his wife, also from Cupar, and four young children lived at South St James Street, a street of 240 households and an average rent of £9.

Notes

1. Housing Quality and Environmental Inequality

1 *The Witness*, 26 Oct 1861.

2 M. W. Flinn ed., *Report on the Sanitary Condition of the Labouring Classes of Gt. Britain* 1842, (by Edwin Chadwick) (Edinburgh edn., 1965), p.280.

3 *The Scotsman* 7 April 1863, p.4.

4 Chadwick, *Report* (1842) 98-99.

5 W. Chambers, *On the Sanitary Condition of the Old Town of Edinburgh* (1840).

6 H. D. Littlejohn, *Report on the Sanitary Condition of Edinburgh* (Edinburgh, 1865) reprinted in full with Appendices in P. Laxton and R. Rodger, *Insanitary City*, p.79.

7 W. T. Gairdner, *Public Health in Relation to Air and Water* (Edinburgh,1862), p.158

8 C. Hamlin, 'Environmental sensibility in Edinburgh 1839-40: the 'fetid irrigation' controversy', *Journal of Urban History,* 20 1994, pp. 311-39; P. J. Smith, 'The foul burns of Edinburgh: public health attitudes and environmental change', *Scottish Geographical Magazine*, 91, (1975), pp.25–37.

9 P. Laxton and R. Rodger, *Insanitary City*, pp.146-55; Littlejohn, *Report*, p.95.

10 Census of Scotland, 1831

11 *The Builder*, 25 May 1861, vol. XIX, no.955, p.349.

12 F. Engels, *The Condition of the Working Class in England,* 1845; 1993 edn., p.47.

13 I. Levitt and T. C. Smout, *The State of the Scottish Working-Class in 1843: A Statistical and Spatial Enquiry based on the Data from the Poor Law Commission Report of 1844* (Edinburgh, 1979), p.174.

14 P. Wright, 'The labour colony system, and its adaptation to our social needs', *Proceedings of the Royal Philosophical Society of Glasgo*w, 26, 1894-95, p.61.

15 *New Edinburgh Almanac* (Edinburgh, 1837), pp.468-80, and (Edinburgh, 1860), pp.749-65.

16 D. Burger, *Practical Religion: David Nasmith and the City Mission Movement 1799-2000*, p.27; see https://www.christianheritageedinburgh.org.uk/category/ecm/

2. Arrested Development

1 A. Dick, *Romanticism and the Gold Standard: Money, Literature and Economic Debate in Britain 1790-1830* (Basingstoke, 2013).

2 P. H. Scott, ed., *The Letters of Malachi Malagrowther.* (Edinburgh, 1981), p.38.

3 See National Library of Scotland (NLS) for historical maps of Edinburgh, https://maps.nls.uk/os/index.html

4 R. Rodger, The transformation of Edinburgh, pp.76-91.

3. Verbal Battlegrounds

1 *The Scotsman*, 15 Feb 1837; 7 Jan and 9 Jan 1839; 25 Dec 1839; 8 Nov 1843; *Edinburgh Evening Courant*, 2 Dec 1847; PP 1844 XVII, First Report of the Inquiry into the State of Large Towns and Populous Districts, 199.

2 P. Laxton, 'This nefarious traffic: livestock and public health in mid-Victorian Edinburgh', in P. Atkins, *Animal Cities: Beastly Urban Histories* (Farnham, 2012), pp.107-72.

3 *The Scotsman*, 13 Feb 1850, p.3 gives many examples of the economies undertaken by the Edinburgh poor regarding food and accommodation.

4 PP 1867-68 XXXIII, Board of Supervision, 22nd Annual Report, pp.v-vi.

5 P. Laxton and R. Rodger, *Insanitary City,* pp.76-80.

6 S. J. Brown, *Thomas Chalmers and the Godly Commonwealth*, pp.91-151; R. A. Cage and E. O. A. Checkland, 'Thomas Chalmers and urban poverty: the St John's experiment in Glasgow 1819-37', *Philosophical Journal*, 13, 1976, pp.39-52. For a later experiment designed to improved inter-denominational collaboration to address poverty see S. J. Brown, 'The Disruption and urban poverty: Thomas Chalmers and the West Port Operation in Edinburgh 1844-47', *Scottish Church History Society,* 20, 1978, pp.65-89.

7 Chalmers' territorial approach was developed in 1838 and announced in a public lecture at St. George's, Edinburgh in January 1839. See *Scottish Guardian,* 25 Jan. 1839, quoted in S. J. Brown, 'The Disruption and urban poverty', p.66.

8 W. P. Alison, 'On the destitution and mortality in some of the large towns in Scotland', *Journal of the Statistical Society of London,* 5, 1842, pp.289-92.

9 C. Hamlin, 'William Pulteney Alison, the Scottish philosophy, and the making of a political medicine' *Journal of History of Medicine and Allied Sciences,* 61:2, 2006, pp.144-86, esp. p.180.

10 *Hansard*, vol.70, 26 July 1843 reported a debate regarding whether those who had ceased to be members of the Established Church of Scotland were entitled to hold public office. I am grateful to Paul Laxton for this reference.

11 C. Brown, 'Religion, class and church growth' in W. H. Fraser and R.J. Norris, eds., *People and Society in Scotland* (Edinburgh, 1990), p.61.

12 R. Mallon, 'A party built on bigotry alone? The Scottish Board of Dissenters and Edinburgh Liberalism, 1834-56', *Scottish Journal of Historical Studies*, 42:2 2021, pp.153-80.

4. Re-thinking the City

1 P. Laxton and R. Rodger, *Insanitary City*, pp.46-68.

2 M. Noble, 'The Common Good', pp.109-49.

3 K. Lynch, *The Image of the City* (Cambridge, Mass.,1960), section III, 'The City Image and its Elements', pp.46-90.

4 17 & 18 Vict. c.91, Lands Valuation (Scotland) Act 1854.

5 17 & 18 Vict. c.80, Registration of Births, Deaths and Marriages (Scotland) Act

6 19 & 20 Vict. c.32, Edinburgh Municipality Extension Act, 1856.

7 See National Library of Scotland, Map Collection, for historical maps of Edinburgh, including the Ordnance Survey First Series 1849-53 https://maps.nls.uk/towns/edinburgh-city.html

8 S. J. Brown,' Beliefs and religions', in T. Griffiths and G. Morton, eds., *A History of Everyday Life in Scotland, 1800 to 1900* (Edinburgh, 2010), pp.116-46.

9 Free Church of Scotland, Committee on Houses for the Working Classes in Connexion with Social Morality, *Report* (Edinburgh, 1862), pp.7-17.

10 Patrick Wilson was a prolific architect particularly designing buildings for the Free Church. An early development at Hopetoun Crescent was a 'tragedy' (J. Gifford' *et al.*, *Buildings of Scotland: Edinburgh*, p.430), a victim of the 1825 financial crisis with only nos. 7/8 and 17/18 completed. Wilson's work included Fountainbridge Free Church (1854); Chalmers Buildings (Fountainbridge, begun 1854); United Presbyterian Church (S. College St., 1856); Cowgate Free Church (1859); Protestant Institute (George IV Bridge, 1860); Chalmers Memorial Free Church (Beaufort Road, 1865). Other work included Tolbooth Parish School, Ramsay Lane (1837); and Dr Guthrie's Original Ragged Industrial School (Mound Place and Ramsay Lane,1850).

11 The management committee included Rev. Blaikie, David Muir (Lord Advocate), Professor Alison, Robert Chambers (publisher), and Francis Brown Douglas (current Lord Provost).

12 Anthony Ashley-Cooper (Lord Ashley (to 1851), then 7th Earl of Shaftesbury (1851-85)).

13 *The Scotsman*, 2 Nov., 1850, p.4.

14 T. Guthrie, *Life of the Rev. Thomas Guthrie*, D.D., (Glasgow, 1873), p.128.

15 L. M. Mair, 'The only friend I have in this world': Ragged School relationships in England and Scotland 1844-1870', unpublished Edinburgh University PhD thesis, 2016.

16 This 'stunting' effect on child development is now widely understood.

17 Subsequently at 9 Alva Street.

18 Anon., 'Old houses in Edinburgh', *Medical Times and Gazette,* 25, 1852, p.349.

19 H. D. Littlejohn, *Report*, p.40, reprinted in Laxton and Rodger, *Insanitary City.*

20 *Edinburgh Evening Courant*, 11 Feb 1850, p.4, Annual Report for 1849.

21 Edinburgh City Archives, ACC 308, Unemployment Relief Fund 1858, Receipts from Subscribers. The donations were equivalent to approximately £118,000 in 2021 prices.

22 *The Builder,* 27 Oct. 1860, p.684.

23 The management committee included Rev Blaikie, David Muir (Lord Advocate), Professor Alison, Robert Chambers (publisher), and Francis Brown Douglas (Lord Provost).

24 Census of Scotland, Edinburgh, 1861.

25 Edinburgh and Leith Post Office Directories, various years. See also Scottish Dictionary of Architects http://www.scottisharchitects.org.uk/architect_full.php?id=200540 Gowans had a habit of living in the properties he built in Edinburgh.

26 *The Builder*, 2 May, 1857, pp.246-47.

27 *The Builder,* 27 Oct. 1860, p.684.

28 NRS, Valuation Rolls, VR100/35/22.

29 See https://canmore.org.uk/collection/1461315 on Rosemount Buildings, Gardner's Crescent.

30 *The Scotsman*, 17 Oct. 1862, p.2. The Rosemount Works were founded in 1857.

31 There were no Edinburgh-born residents in Pilrig Model Buildings in 1861.

32 Limited Liability Act, 1855, 18 & 19 Vict c.33.

33 Census of Scotland, Edinburgh, 1861.

34 J. N. Tarn, *Five Per Cent Philanthropy: an Account of Housing in Urban Areas between 1840 and 1914* (Cambridge, 1973).

35 The 'assessed rent' officially declared to the Edinburgh Assessor in 1860 is used here. This varies slightly from Littlejohn's *Report* (Table X) for the lowest rent.

36 B. R Mitchell and P. Deane, *Abstract of British Historical Statistics* (Cambridge, 1971), pp.456-57.

Notes

37 Founded in 1832 by David Naismith continues to provide support through Foodbanks and the Care Van, working in association with the Bethany Trust.

38 *The Scotsman*, 22 Sept. 1858, p.3.

5. A Change of Tone

1 *The Scotsman*, 2 Feb. 1850, p.3; also *The Scotsman*, 6, 9, and 13 Feb. 1850.

2 S. Cohen, *Folk Devils and Moral Panics: the Creation of Mods and Rockers* (London, 1972).

3 *The Scotsman*, 13 Feb. 1850.

4 *The Evening News*, Sept. 1853. Source: R. Foulis, *Old Houses in Edinburgh and their Inhabitants* (1852).

5 K. Leask, *Hugh Miller* (Edinburgh 1896), pp.96-118 for an engaging account of Miller in Edinburgh.

6 H. Miller, quoted in R. Pipes, *The Colonies of Stockbridge* (Edinburgh, 1984), 9.

7 J. Begg, speech to Scottish Social Reform Association, 18 Jan. 1850, quoted in J. Clark, *Life of James Begg*, p.7.

8 Hugh Gilzean Reid, see Appendix 4.

9 J. S. Mill, *On Liberty*, Part I, p.306. Both Self-Help and Origin of Species were published by another Edinburgh graduate John Murray.

10 The Industrial and Provident Societies Partnership Act, 1852 (Slaney's Act), 15 and 16 Vict. c.31; D. Lambourne, *Slaney's Act and the Christian Socialists* (Boston, Lincs. 2008).

11 Some protection to small businesses was also available through the Joint Stock Companies Act, 1844 (7 & 8 Vict. c.110) and Limited Liability Act, 1855 (18 & 19 Vict. c.133); S. Pollard, 'Nineteenth century cooperation from community building to shopkeeping', in A. Brigg and J. Saville, eds., *Essays in Labour History* (London, 1967), pp.74-112.

6. Building Cooperation

1 J. Kinloch and J. Butt, *History of the Scottish Cooperative Wholesale Society Limited* (Glasgow, 1981), pp.1-2. Govan Victualling Society (est. 1800), Lennoxtown Friendly Victualling Society (1812), Balfron Equitable and Victualling Society (1815), Larkhall Victualling Society (1821), Galashiels Provision Store and Hawick Chartist Store (1839). See also J. A. Kinloch, 'The Scottish Co-operative Wholesale Society 1868-1918', Strathclyde University PhD thesis, 1976.

2 *Report of the Committee of the Working Classes of Edinburgh on the Present Overcrowded and Uncomfortable State of their Dwelling Houses*, p3. They ten were: George Crombie (engineer); Alexander Fraser (blacksmith); Robert Watson (warehouseman);

William Davidson (coach-builder); Allan Scott (wheelwright); Thomas Peters (joiner); David Tennent (post office clerk); David Butler (teacher); George Mackay (printer) with Alexander Macpherson, secretary.

3 W. Chambers, *Social Science Tracts* (London 1860). Chambers was Lord Provost (1865-69) and an ardent supporter of the City Improvement Scheme, 1867 to demolish insanitary housing and replace it with more generous space and amenities.

4 W. Maxwell, ed., *First Fifty Years of St Cuthbert's Cooperative Association Limited 1859-1909* (Edinburgh, 1909).

5 I. MacDougall, ed., *The Minutes of Edinburgh Trades Council 1859-73* (Edinburgh 1968), p.xv. Earlier individual trades unions in Edinburgh included bookbinders (1822), plasterers (1827), printers (1826), cabinetmakers (1836).

6 The union meetings were held at Burden's Coffee House, 129 High Street. Both Borrowman and Caw subsequently lost their jobs due to their union activities. Saturday was preferred by employers as pay day because it ensured that workers would turn up for work.

7 Minute of Meeting of Edinburgh Trades Council, 22 Nov. 1859, in I. MacDougall, ed., *Minutes,* p.23.

8 A. Allen, *Building Early Modern Edinburgh: A Social History of Craftwork and Incorporation* (Edinburgh, 2019); J. Colston, *The Incorporated Trades of Edinburgh* (Edinburgh, 1891), pp.1-144.

9 I. MacDougall, ed., *Minutes,* p.xxxvii.

10 *The Scotsman*, 25 May 1860, Editorial. This was an early instance of using Registrar General's statistics to make a broader argument.

11 W. Pickard, *The Member for Scotland: A Life of Duncan McLaren* Edinburgh 2011), pp.167-74.

12 J. Begg, *Happy Homes*, p.50

13 H. G. Reid, 'Building trades disputes in Scotland 1861-2', *Transactions of the National Association for the Promotion of Social Science (*London, 1863), p.722.

14 *The Scotsman*, 25 May 1860, p.2.

15 *The Scotsman*, 5 Mar. p.2.

16 *The Times*, 15 Apr 1861, p.7.

17 See P. Laxton and R. Rodger, *Insanitary City,* pp.80-3. There had been previous building collapses however, though none with the same number of fatalities

18 Free Church of Scotland, Committee on Houses for the Working Classes in Connexion with Social Morality, *Report*, (Edinburgh, 1862), pp.7-17.

19 Report of the Committee of the Working Classes, Appendix III, Report of the Sub-Committee on Statistics.

Notes

20 R. Rodger, 'Industrial city: Edinburgh 1800-1914' in B. Edwards and P. Jenkins, eds.,'*Edinburgh: the Making of a Capital City* (Edinburgh, 2005), pp.85-102.

21 R. Q. Gray, *The Labour Aristocracy in Nineteenth Century Edinburgh* (Oxford, 1976) provides the best account of labour relationships.

7. Structural Strength

1 *The Scotsman*, 10 Dec. 1880, p.3. The building yard soon after moved to Balmoral Place, Stockbridge, and then to Annandale Street in 1911. The office moved to 46 Cockburn Street in 1862 and later to Castle Street.

2 *The Scotsman*, 10 Dec. 1880, p.3.

3 P. Laxton and R. Rodger, *Insanitary City*, pp.172-88.

4 *The Scotsman*, 30 Nov. 1861, p.7.

5 NRS, GD327/505/1 and 505/2.

6 The Directors for the first year, all building tradesmen, were David Rintoul (Chairman), John Ogilvie (Treasurer), James Colville (Manager, full time, wages 5 shillings a week above current masons' wages); William Mill (Secretary), James Collins, Thomas Morgan, James Earshman, John W. Syme, David Lockerby, George Weddell, John Duncan, Robert Kerr, David Hardie, George Herbert, John Baird and George McKenzie.

7 J. Begg, *Happy Homes*, p.26.

8 *The Scotsman*, 7 Apr. 1863, p.4.

9 *The Scotsman*, 7 Apr. 1863, p.4.

10 NRS RS27/2354.126, feu disposition, 11 Sep 1861. See also R. Pipes, *The Colonies of Stockbridge* pp.16-26 for the background to the Glenogle site.

8. From Strength to Strength

1 NRS GD327/507/1, ECBC 2nd Annual Report, 25 May 1863.

2 The average dividend in the first 20 years was 10.5%.

3 *The Scotsman*, 10 Dec. 1880, p.3.

4 Merchant Company Archives, Drumdryan Chartulary, vo.2; NRS GD327/489; 4th Annual Report May 1865; J. Begg, *Happy Homes for Working Men* (Edinburgh 1872 edn.), Appendix III.

5 NRS/GD327/489, Quarterly Meeting of Shareholders, 27 Nov. 1865. When profits were in the range 5-8%, then the distribution was 5%, and remainder to the Contingent fund; when profits 9-11%, then 7.5% distributed; and when over 11%, then 10% distributed with the balance to the contingent fund.

6 NRS Valuation Rolls/100/33-37. The average rental refers to privately rented properties and excludes properties owned by companies, institutions, public bodies and owner-occupied homes.

7 This time the cavity was filled with a stone glass bottle containing Begg's pamphlet on working men's houses, his portrait, and copies of the Edinburgh newspapers.

8 *The Scotsman*, 8 Mar, 1862, p.3.

9 Based on J. Begg, *Happy Homes for Working Men* (Edinburgh 1872 edn.) Appendix III.

10 ECBC 24th Annual Report, 1885.

11 *Edinburgh Evening Courant*, 6 Jan. 1862, p.2, brackets added. See also J. Begg, *Happy Homes*, p.37 for the reference to 'cold reception'.

12 J. Begg, *Happy Homes*, pp.43-4.

13 ECBC, 7th Annual Report, 1868. Salmond, Earlston and Pitlochry Places.

14 R. Rodger, *The Transformation of Edinburgh*, pp.211-21, 374; Edinburgh City Archives ACC 282, James Walker's Trust, Feu Contract and Disposition, 29 Aug. 1867.

15 ECBC Annual Reports, 1867 and 1868.

16 ECBC Annual Report, 1868.

17 ECBC Annual Report 1871.

18 ECBC Annual Report, 1871.

19 ECBC Annual Report 1869.

20 J. Begg, *Happy Homes*, Appendix III. Shops (17) and houses under construction (42) are excluded.

21 ECBC Annual Report, May 1871.

22 NRS, Valuation Roll, Edinburgh 1910, VR100/270. Miss Hamilton's portfolio was managed by John Hamilton, 2 Craiglockhart Terrace.

23 Closer inspection reveals larger, coarser stonework, and no external staircase access.

24 NRS, SRO BT2/284 Memorandum of Association of the Industrial Co-operative Building Company (Limited), 8 Apr 1868 and bankruptcy CS318/49/67; Letter from A. F. W. Fingzies to Wallace and Pennell, WS, 27 Feb 1901; Inventory and Valuation, 6 Mar. 1901; Sederunt Book, folio.32.

25 See R. Rodger, *The Transformation of Edinburgh*, pp.69-76 for an explanation of feuing and land prices.

26 Census of Scotland, 1871. Of these 225 households, 23% had female heads in the 8 Lauriston building associations.

27 R. Rodger, *The Transformation of Edinburgh*, pp. 166-73

9. Building Phases

1 NRS GD1/777/2, 15th Annual Report, May 1876.

2 R. Rodger, 'Structural instability in the Scottish building industry 1820-80', *Construction History*, 2, 1986, pp.48-60; R. Rodger, 'Speculative builders and the structure of the Scottish building industry 1860-1914', *Business History, 2*1, 1979, pp.226-46, DOI: 10.1080/00076797900000029

3 NRS GD327/508, handwritten memo.

4 NRS GD327/489, 16th Annual Report, 1877.

5 NRS GD327/508/1 Kemp papers. Suggestions affecting the future of the Edinburgh Co-operative Building Company with reference to comments in 15th Annual Report 1876.

6 NRS Register of Sasines, (RS) 108/820.57, fue disposition, trustee Robert McNaughton to trusteees of the ECBC, 23 Oct 1877. I am indebted to Rose Pipes for this information.

7 NRS RS108/230.34, feu disposition, 29 July 1871.

8 NRS RS108/539.184, 14 May 1875; RS108/333.89 13 Jan 1872; and fifteen other feu dispositions for Barnton Terrace.

9 ECBC 18th Annual Report 1879.

10 R. Rodger, 'The Victorian building industry and the housing of the Scottish working class', in M. Doughty, ed., *Building the Industrial City*, (Leicester 1986), p.181.

11 Census of Scotland, Schedules, Edinburgh Public Library, 1871, 1881, and 1891.

12 ECBC 23rd Annual Report 1884.

13 He received an honorarium of £100 in 1890, worth approximately £11,200 in 2021 prices. James Colville was one of ten members (six of whom were Free Church ministers) who formed the platform party which announced the foundaton of the ECBC on St Andrew's day, 1861. He introduced the first speaker, publisher and later Lord Provost, William Chambers.

14 ECBC 29th Annual Report 1890.

15 ECBC 28th Annual Report 1889.

16 ECBC 25th and 26th Annual Reports 1886, 1887.

17 ECBC 30th Annual Report 1891.

18 NRS GD327/499 Draft Minutes of the Special Committee to consider the proposal to increase the capital out of reserve funds 15 May 1899, and Letter from D. W. Kemp to Andrew Salmond, Chairman ECBC, 14 May 1899.

19 ECBC 52nd Annual Report 1913. In 1908-10 a sale of feu duties produced £3500.

20 Note: the dates of site acquisition, planned building and actual construction vary slightly.

21 ECBC 31st Annual Report 1892.

22 ECBC 42nd Annual Report, 1903.

23 ECBC 42nd Annual Report, 1903. Planning approval was given on 29 May 1903.

24 NRS Valuation Roll, VR

25 R. Rodger, 'The Victorian building industry and the housing of the Scottish working class', in M. Doughty, ed., *Building the Industrial City* (Leicester U.P., 1986), pp.151-206.

26 ECBC 50th Annual Report.

27 ECBC 51st Annual Report.

10. War, Depression and Decline

1 City of Edinburgh Charity Organisation Society, *Report on the Physical Condition of Fourteen Hundred Schoolchildren in the City* (Edinburgh 1906).

2 PP 1917-18 XIV, Cd.8731, Royal Commission on the Housing of the Industrial Population of Scotland, Rural and Urban, p.387.

3 J. Melling. 'Clydeside housing and the evolution of State rent control', in J. Melling, ed., *Housing, Social Policy and the State* (London, 1980), pp. 139-67.

4 N. Milnes, *A Study of Industrial Edinburgh and the Surrounding Area,* vol.1, (1936), pp.170-74.

5 S. Robb, 'Ebenezer MacRae and interwar housing in Edinburgh', *Book of the Old Edinburgh Club,* 13, 2017, pp.43-78

6 A. O'Carroll, 'The influence of local authorities on owner occupation: Edinburgh and Glasgow 1914-1939', *Planning Perspectives,* 11:1, 1996, pp.55-72; A. O'Carroll, 'Social homes, private homes', the re-shaping of Scottish housing 1914-39', in M. Glendinning and D. Watters, eds., *Homebuilders: Mactaggart & Mickel and the Scottish Housebuilding Industry* (Edinburgh, 1999), pp.211-23.

7 D. McCrone, *Understanding Scotland: the Sociology of a Stateless Nation* (London, 1992), p.157.

8 NRS GD327/506/1, Kemp to Salmond, 14 June 1901The words in square brackets were struck from his speech. .

9 NRS GD327/496/3

11. Who Lived in the Colonies?

1 H. G. Reid, *Housing the Poor. An Example in Co-operation* (London 1895), pp.62-9.

2 J.W.R. Whitehand, 'Fringe belts: a neglected aspect of urban geography', *Transactions of the Institute of British Geographers*, 41, 1967, pp.223-33.

3 W. Pickard, *The Member for Scotland: A Life of Duncan McLaren* (Edinburgh, 2011).

4 G. R. Boyer, 'Living standards 1860-1939', in R. Floud and P. Johnson, eds., *The Cambridge Economic History of Modern Britain,* vol.2, *Economic Maturity, 1860-1939,* p.284, Table 11.2.

5 R. Rodger, 'Making the Census count: revealing Edinburgh 1760-1900', *Journal of Scottish Historical Studies,* 40:2, 2020, esp. pp.142-48 and Table 3. See DOI: 10.3366/jshs.2020.0300; P. J. Smith, 'Slum clearance as an instrument of sanitary reform: the flawed vision of Edinburgh's first slum clearance scheme', *Planning Perspectives,* 9, 1994, pp.1-27.

6 Data abstract from microfilm copies of the Census, 1871, 1881, and 1891, and supplemented by I-CeM Data for 1901. It must be noted that, unlike England, the Census of Scotland for 1911 is not available, nor will the 1921 Census be available, on the same basis as in England. See R. Rodger, 'Making the Census count', pp.134-48.

7 Municipal Elections Amendment (Scotland) Act 1881, *PP 44 & 45 Vict. c.13.*

8 Though also eligible to be Lord Provost, women were nonetheless still prevented from acting as JPs or baillies until 1920. See Breitenbach, 'Edinburgh Suffragists', p.66.

9 Conjugal Rights (Scotland) Amendment Act, 1861, c. 86, Section 16.

10 If the husband made 'a reasonable provision for the support and maintenance of the wife' from any post-marriage property obtained by his wife he could continue to have some control of her property.

11 NRS GD327/490, Annual Reports.

12 M. Pember Reeves, *Round about a Pound a Week* (London 1914) pp.75-93, 132-45.

12. Legacies

1 See https://www.cala.co.uk/homes-for-sale/scotland/edinburgh/cammo-meadows-edinburgh/ Cala wrongly attribute ECBC development to 1850.

2 The only exceptions were the Ferry Road and Balgreen developments, and the exceptional Craigleith Road.

3 NRS GD327/506/1, Letter from D. W. Kemp to Salmond, 14 June 1901, f.3.

4 NRS GD327/488 Tabular Statement.

5 NRS, BT2/1970/548/79/4, E. B. Contractors, shareholders list.

6 English shareholders accounted for 7.8% Source: NRS GD327/496/3 Houses Rented 1943.

Bibliography

Alison, W.P., 'On the destitution and mortality in some of the large towns in Scotland', *Journal of the Statistical Society of London*, 5, 1842, pp.289-92

Allen, A., *Building Early Modern Edinburgh: A Social History of Craftwork and Incorporation* (Edinburgh, 2019)

Begg, J., *Happy Homes for Working Men and How to Get Them* (Edinburgh, 1866) and 1872 edn.

Boyer, G. R., 'Living standards 1860-1939', in R. Floud and P. Johnson, eds., *The Cambridge Economic History of Modern Britain,* vol.2, *Economic Maturity, 1860-1939,* (Cambridge, 2004), Table 11.2

Breitenbach, E., 'Edinburgh Suffragists: exercising the franchise at local level', *Book of the Old Edinburgh Club*, 15, 2019, 63-60

Brown, C., 'Religion, class and church growth', in W. H. Fraser and R. J. Morris, eds., *People and Society in Scotland* (Edinburgh, 1990), pp.310-35

Brown, S. J., 'The Disruption and urban poverty: Thomas Chalmers and the West Port Operation in Edinburgh 1844-47', *Scottish Church History Society,* 20, 1978, pp.65-89

Brown, S.J., *Thomas Chalmers and the Godly Commonwealth*, (Oxford, 1983), pp.91-151

Brown, S. J., 'Beliefs and religions', in T. Griffiths and G. Morton, eds., *A History of Everyday Life in Scotland, 1800 to 1900* (Edinburgh, 2010), pp.116-46

Burger, D., *Practical Religion: David Nasmith and the City Mission Movement 1799-2000*

Cage, R. A. and E. O. A. Checkland, 'Thomas Chalmers and urban poverty: the St John's experiment in Glasgow 1819-37", *Philosophical Journal*, 13, 1976, pp.39-52

Chambers, W., *Social Science Tracts* (London, 1860)

Clark, J., *Life of James Begg* (no date)

Cohen, S., *Folk Devils and Moral Panics: the Creation of Mods and Rockers* (London, 1972)

Colston, J., *The Incorporated Trades of Edinburgh* (Edinburgh, 1891)

Dick, A., *Romanticism and the Gold Standard: Money, Literature, and Economic Debate in Britain 1790-1830* (Basingstoke, 2013)

Engels, F. *The Condition of the Working Class in England,* 1845 (1993 edn.)

Flinn, M.W., ed., *Report on the Sanitary Condition of the Labouring Classes of Gt. Britain 1842* (by Edwin Chadwick) (Edinburgh edn., 1965)

Gairdner, W.T., *Public Health in Relation to Air and Water* (Edinburgh, 1862)

Gray, R. Q., *The Labour Aristocracy in Nineteenth Century Edinburgh* (Oxford, 1976)

Guthrie, T., *Life of the Rev. Thomas Guthrie, D.D.,* (Glasgow, 1873)

Hamlin, C., 'Environmental sensibility in Edinburgh 1839-40: the "fetid irrigation" controversy', *Journal of Urban History*, 20, 1994, pp.311-39

Hamlin, C., 'William Pulteney Alison, the Scottish philosophy, and the making of a political medicine'*Journal of History of Medicine and Allied Sciences*, 61:2, 2006, pp.144-86

Kinloch, J. and J. Butt, *History of the Scottish Cooperative Wholesale Society Limited* (Glasgow, 1981)

Lambourne, D., *Slaney's Act and the Christian Socialists* (Boston, Lincs., 2008)

Laxton, P., 'This nefarious traffic: livestock and public health in mid-Victorian Edinburgh', in P. Atkins, ed.,'*Animal Cities: Beastly Urban Histories* (Farnham 2012), pp.107-72

Laxton, P. and R. Rodger, *Insanitary City: Henry Littlejohn and the Condition of Edinburgh* (Lancaster, 2012)

Leask, K., *Hugh Miller* (Edinburgh 1896), pp.96-118

Levitt, I. and T. C. Smout, *The State of the Scottish Working-Class in 1843: A Statistical and Spatial Enquiry based on the Data from the Poor Law Commission Report of 1844* (Edinburgh, 1979)

Littlejohn, H. D., *Report on the Sanitary Condition of Edinburgh* (Edinburgh, 1865) reprinted with Appendices in P. Laxton and R. Rodger, *Insanitary City* (Edinburgh, 2012)

Lynch, K., *The Image of the City* (Cambridge, Mass.,1960) section 3, 'The City Image and its Elements', pp.46-90

MacDougall, I., ed., *The Minutes of Edinburgh Trades Council 1859-73* (Edinburgh, 1968)

Mallon, R., 'A party built on bigotry alone? The Scottish Board of Dissenters and Edinburgh Liberalism, 1834-56', *Scottish Journal of Historical Studies*, 42:2 2021, pp.153-80

Maxwell, W., ed., *First Fifty Years of St Cuthbert's Cooperative Association Limited 1859-1909* (Edinburgh, 1909)

McCrone, D., *Understanding Scotland: the Sociology of a Stateless Nation* (London, 1992),

Melling, J., 'Clydeside housing and the evolution of State rent control', in J. Melling, ed., *Housing, Social Policy and the State* (London, 1980), pp.139-67

Mill, J. S. *On Liberty*, Part I, p.306

Milnes, N., *A Study of Industrial Edinburgh and the Surrounding Area*, vol.1, (Edinburgh, 1936) pp.170-74.

Mitchell, B. R. and P. Deane, *Abstract of British Historical Statistics* (Cambridge, 1971)

O'Carroll, A., 'The influence of local authorities on owner occupation: Edinburgh and Glasgow 1914-1939', *Planning Perspectives*, 11:1, 1996, pp.55-72

O'Carroll, A., 'Social homes, private homes', the re-shaping of Scottish housing 1914-39', in M. Glendinning and D. Watters, eds., *Homebuilders: Mactaggart & Mickel and the Scottish Housebuilding Industry* (Edinburgh, 1999), pp.211-23.

Pember Reeves, M., *Round about a Pound a Week* (London, 1914)

Pickard, W., *The Member for Scotland: A Life of Duncan McLaren* (Edinburgh, 2011)

Pipes, R., *The Colonies of Stockbridge* (Edinburgh, 1984)

Pollard, S., 'Nineteenth century cooperation: from community building to shopkeeping', in A. Briggs and J. Saville, eds.,'*Essays in Labour History*'(London, 1967), pp.74-112.

Reid, H. G., 'Building trades disputes in Scotland 1861-2', *Transactions of the National Association for the Promotion of Social Science* (London, 1863), p.722.

Reid, H. G., *Housing the Poor. An Example in Co-operation* (London, 1895), pp.62-9.

Robb, S., 'Ebenezer MacRae and interwar housing in Edinburgh', *Book of the Old Edinburgh Club*, 13, 2017, pp.43-78.

Rodger, R., 'Speculative builders and the structure of the Scottish building industry 1860-1914', *Business History*, 21, 1979, pp.226-46, https://doi.org/10.1080/00076797900000029

Rodger, R., 'Structural instability in the Scottish building industry 1820-80', *Construction History*, 2, 1986, pp.48-60; https://ur.booksc.eu/ireader/48155018

Rodger, R., 'The Victorian building industry and the housing of the Scottish working class', in M. Doughty, ed., *Building the Industrial City*, (Leicester, 1986), pp.151-206

Rodger, R., *The Transformation of Edinburgh: Land, Property and Trust in the Nineteenth Century* (Cambridge, 2001; pbk. 2008) Winner: Frank Watson Prize in Scottish History

Rodger, R., 'Industrial city: Edinburgh 1800-1914' in B. Edwards and P. Jenkins, eds., *Edinburgh: the Making of a Capital City* (Edinburgh, 2005), pp.85-102

Rodger, R., 'Making the Census count: revealing Edinburgh 1760-1900', *Journal of Scottish Historical Studies*, 40:2, 2020, pp.134-48, https://doi.org/10.3366/jshs.2020.0300

Rodger, R., 'Property and inequality: housing dynamics in a nineteenth-century city', *Economic History Review*, 2022 https://doi.org/10.1111/ehr.13138

Scott, P. H., ed., *The Letters of Malachi Malagrowther*. (Edinburgh 1981)

Smith, P. J., 'The foul burns of Edinburgh: public health attitudes and environmental change', *Scottish Geographical Magazine*, 91, 1975, pp.25–37

Smith, P. J., 'Slum clearance as an instrument of sanitary reform: the flawed vision of Edinburgh's first slum clearance scheme', *Planning Perspectives*, 9, 1994, pp.1-27.

Tarn, J. N., *Five Per Cent Philanthropy: an Account of Housing in Urban Areas between 1840 and 1914* (Cambridge, 1973).

Whitehand, J. W. R. 'Fringe belts: a neglected aspect of urban geography', *Transactions of the Institute of British Geographers*, 41, 1967, pp.223-33.

Acknowledgements

NO PUBLICATION exists without many debts and *Happy Homes: Cooperation, Community and the Edinburgh Colonies* is no exception. Amongst those to whom I'm indebted are the late Helen Clark and Rose Pipes with whom I collaborated to present an exhibition (2000) on 'The Colonies' in the City Art Centre. Part of that exhibition involved a computer terminal where the data mining of the microfilm versions of the Censuses of Edinburgh by myself and Sheila Hamilton was rendered digitally searchable to visitors by Alex Moseley. It was a novel, exciting feature which brought the past into the present for visitors and pointed one way to a digital future which foregrounded historical records.

Throughout Scotland, Local Studies librarians deal valiantly with an under-resourced, under-acknowledged and under-appreciated service and the Edinburgh Room in the Central Library on George IV Bridge is no exception. My thanks go to them over many years of cheerful help and advice. A particular resource, enjoyed by many and extremely helpful as far as my research is concerned, is the online Capital Collections, the digital database of some of the 100,000 images held by Edinburgh Libraries (https://www.capitalcollections.org.uk) some of which date back to the birth of photography.

The Map Library of the National Library of Scotland is another gem of international repute. Of international repute with one of the largest digitised map collections anywhere. I have relied on their resources to an extraordinary degree, and particularly on the expert advice of the Senior Map Curator, Chris Fleet. For digital access to the historical Census of Scotland 1851-1901 I am particularly grateful to Matthew Woollard and the UK Data Archive.

My co-author of *Insanitary City,* Paul Laxton, has provided his usual acute comments, and Bob Morris and Rebecca Madgin have offered encouragement, and support. Many others have made suggestions, and shared their own ideas – Ignacio Ferreras, Andrew Johnstone, and Hetty Lancaster particularly – and the acute memberships of the many local history societies neighbourhood organisations that I've addressed over the years, including the Old Edinburgh Club – Edinburgh's local history society.

Finally, many people kept me going as the scale of the research expanded. Clan Rodger, past and present, and especially Susan, Anna and Euan, put up with me while I immersed myself in volumes of information, a fraction of which only are incorporated here. I owe much to Sean Bradley, one of my most longstanding and enthusiastic supporters, and 'midwife' to this volume, and Derek Rodger – no relation! Both were very patient with me as we moved into the production stages of this book. I value again the use of photos by John Reiach. To you all, your input is deeply appreciated.

Not least, a warm 'thanks' to the Board and Management team at Scotmid. Their awareness of the cooperative dimension to the history of contemporary Edinburgh in the form of a financial contribution towards publication has been a key factor in making this book affordable.

Index

A

Abbeyhill 50, 51, 66, 79, 88, 89, 93, 94, 95, 96, 106, 110, 114, 130, 141, 144, 154, 186
Abbeyhill glass works 144
Alderbank Gardens, Place, Terrace 114, 123, 169, 162, 186
Alison, Prof. William P. 13, 21, 29, 31, 39, 171, 172, 173
Almondbank 114, 160
Alva Place 93
Annual General Meetings 101, 112, 157
annuitant/pensioner 84, 110, 128, 139, 140-1, 144, 154, 157
architecture 25, 39, 40, 43, 65, 152, 164, 166
Argyll Terrace 90, 93
Articles of Association 69, 151
Ashley Buildings – see 'model' dwellings
Ashley, Lord (7th Earl of Shaftesbury) 39-41, 107
Ashley Terrace 107, 109, 114
Atholl Terrace 162

B

Baird, Sir William J.G. 116, 118, 147
Balgreen 109, 117, 120, 128, 133, 147, 161, 163
Balgreen Avenue 160
Balgreen Road 116, 118-20, 161
Saughtonhall Drive 116
Balmoral Place 93, 159, 175
bankruptcy 26, 35, 99, 105, 107
Barnton Terrace 102, 103, 107, 177
Bedford Street 72, 75, 165, 167
Beechwood Terrace 103, 159
beehive 133
Begg, Rev. Dr. James 10, 11, 31, 36, 52, 56, 63, 64, 72, 79, 83, 84, 131, 143, 155, 164, 174
Begg's Buildings – see 'model' dwellings
Bell, Dr. George 13
Blackfriars Wynd 12, 13, 20
Blackhall station 103
Blaikie, Rev. Dr. William Garden 37, 38, 39, 164
Bonnington 87
Brand Place 48, 51-2,
Breadalbane Cottages 93, 159
Breadalbane Terrace 93, 159
breakfast missions 42
Bright, John 63, 132
Brighton Street Chapel 59, 63, 69
Bristo Street 72
Brougham Street 87
Buccleuch Street Hall 59, 64
building industry 7, 92, 99, 106, 107, 112, 119, 125, 156, 157, 177, 178, 179

building societies 96, 124, 128
building trades 25, 52, 61, 63-66, 72, 75, 79, 84-5, 94, 106-7, 110-11, 129, 132, 138-41, 144, 147, 153, 155
bungalow 126-7
Burntisland 151, 152

C

Caledonian Brewery 103
Caledonian Distillery 66
Caledonian Railway 88, 103, 104, 114
Caledonian Terrace 89
Calton 36, 42
Canongate 13, 20, 49, 66, 88, 123, 168
Canonmills 32, 75
Carlyle Place 93
Castle Terrace 26, 166
Castle Hill 21, 41-2
Causewayside 72, 155
Chadwick, Edwin 13, 14, 43, 170, 181
Chalmers Buildings – see 'model' dwellings
Chalmers, Rev. Dr. Thomas 31, 32, 43, 164, 165, 171
Chambers, William 13-15, 60, 63, 69
charitable organisations 20-1, 29, 31, 42, 53
Charity Organisation Society 123
Edinburgh City Mission (ECM) 21

185

Night Asylum for the Houseless 41-2
Society for the Relief of Indigent Old Men 21
cholera 16, 24, 27, 35, 41
churches
    Catholic 21
    Church of Scotland 13, 21, 31-2, 35, 65
    Free Church of Scotland 20-1, 32, 36-8, 41, 43, 48, 55-6, 64, 164-66
Clermiston Buildings 48
closes, wynds 13, 19, 20, 22, 41, 48, 56, 64, 131, 133
Cobden, Richard 63, 132
Cobden Terrace 159
Cockburn Street 72, 175
Colville, James 8, 75, 85, 96, 102, 110, 132, 133, 138, 153, 165, 168, 176, 178
companies
    North British and Mercantile Insurance Company 103
    North British Railway Company 116
    North British Rubber Company 66, 105
cooperative movement 46, 58-61, 64, 66, 72-3, 94, 110
    St Cuthbert's Cooperative Society 60, 64, 72
Co-operative Plasterers' Society 72
Cornhill Terrace 114, 146
Cowgate 12, 13, 20, 24, 41, 42, 53, 123
Craigentinny 16
Cranston, Robert 51
Croall's Buildings 48

D

Daisy Terrace 103-4, 107, 159
Dalry colonies 27, 54, 66, 67, 79, 83, 87-93, 99, 103, 105, 110, 132, 136, 139, 141, 145, 147, 151, 161
Darwin, Charles *The Origin of Species* 57, 59
death rates 63
Disruption (of Church of Scotland) 28, 32, 36, 39, 164, 165, 171
dividend (ECBC) 7, 69, 79, 80, 87, 89, 92, 94, 96, 100, 101, 112, 126, 129, 140, 148, 155, 156, 157
Douglas Terrace 159, 162
Douglas, Francis Brown (Lord Provost) 132, 164
Duncan, John 120, 176
Dundee 18, 123
Dunrobin Place 93

E

Earlston Place 99, 159
East Restalrig Terrace 114, 117, 146
Edinburgh Association for Building Houses for the Working Classes 53
Edinburgh Association for Improving the Condition of the Poor 53
Edinburgh Building Contractors 128
Edinburgh City Mission 21, 53
Edinburgh Cooperative Building Company 7, 8, 11, 30, 46, 48, 49, 52, 55, 64, 73, 83, 131, 151, 164, 165, 167

management 72, 81, 99, 107-8, 124, 128, 147, 149, 152, 157, 166
Memorandum of Association 62, 65, 72, 154, 165, 167, 168
Park: Glendevon Park 132, 160
Glenogle Park 132
Merchiston Park 6, 46, 132, 147
Norton Park 88, 132, 134, 138, 140, 159
Restalrig Park 87, 89, 94, 101, 112, 114 116, 132, 159
Shaftesbury Park 107-11, 114, 116-17, 120, 133, 147
Edinburgh Corporation/Town Council 84, 116, 123, 124, 125, 128, 129
Edinburgh Improvement Trust 164
Edinburgh National Society for Women's Suffrage (1867) 141
Edinburgh Society for the Relief of Indigent Old Men 21
Elmwood Terrace 103, 171, 173, 176
Eyemouth 129

F

family 8, 16, 18, 24, 29, 39, 41, 48, 80, 84, 117, 132-3, 143-4, 151, 154, 164-8
Ferniehill 86, 87
Ferry Road 81, 85, 86, 87, 91, 99, 135, 136, 137, 138, 141, 144, 145
feu, feu duties 26-7, 69, 75, 79, 87, 89, 92, 95, 100,

102, 105, 111, 114, 118, 120, 155
Fife 135, 136, 165, 168
Fingzies, A.&W. 94, 114, 115
Fisherrow 152
Flower Colonies 33, 104, 106, 137
Foulis, Dr. Robert 41
founders (of ECBC) 66, 132, 151, 155, 156, 157, 164
Fountainbridge 42, 45, 59, 60, 66, 72, 105, 166
Free Church of Scotland – see churches

G

Gairdner, Dr. William T. 15
Galashiels 59, 129
Gardner's Crescent 26, 44, 97, 156
George IV Bridge 185
George Mill 110, 167
George Square 164
Gillis' Buildings 48
Gladstone Terrace 87
Gladstone's Buildings 48
Glasgow 18, 20-11, 31, 105-6, 123, 156, 165
Glendevon Place – see also Balgreen 116, 118, 121
Glenogle Road 9, 69, 79
Gorgie 102, 103, 106
Gowans, James 44, 46, 51, 69, 166
Grassmarket 20, 41
Guthrie, Dr Thomas 41

H

Haig, James (whisky distillers) 69, 75, 79
Hamilton Place 48, 110, 168
Hawthornbank Place, Terrace 79, 81, 82,

85, 93, 99, 135, 136, 137, 138, 141, 145
Haymarket 27, 66, 67, 87, 88
Henderson Place 81, 85, 93, 101
Heriot's Trustees 27, 84, 86
Heriot's Hospital 84, 86
Hermitage Hill 109, 112–117, 120
  Cornhill Terrace 114, 120, 146, 160, 163
  East Restalrig Terrace 114, 117, 146, 160, 163
  Restalrig Road 94, 114
  Ryehill Avenue, Gardens, Grove, Place, Terrace 114, 120, 146-48, 163
  Summerfield Place (ECBC) 114
High School Yards 24
High Street – see also closes, wynds 13, 15, 20, 40, 65, 131
highlanders 20, 31
Hillhousefield 72
Hollybank Terrace 111, 114
Housing Acts (1919, 1923, 1924) 123-25
housing, insanitary 29, 31, 39, 46, 53, 69, 153
housing market 25, 53, 123, 124
Hugh Miller Place 57, 74, 79, 84, 94, 146, 166

I

Improvement Act (1867) 133
Improvement Trusts 106, 164, 133
incomes 7, 22, 28, 39, 52, 106, 123, 126
  salaries 22, 110
  pensions, annuities 84,

110, 140, 157
  rents 7, 52, 94, 96, 112, 123, 125, 145
Industrial Cooperative Building Company 114, 115
Industrial Museum (Royal Scottish Museum) 11, 69
Industrial Cooperative Building Company 94-5, 114-6
Industrial Road 94, 116, 151
industry 7, 16, 31, 63, 66, 75, 92, 99, 101, 103, 105-7, 112, 114, 119, 125, 147-8, 156-7
inequality 13, 16, 18, 20-3, 83-5, 108, 120, 138, 142
Irish/Ireland 19, 20, 31, 35, 135, 136
  immigration 19, 20
  in Old Town 19
Ivy Terrace 104, 156, 159

K

Kemp, D. W. 80, 111, 112, 126, 132, 166
Kemp Place 110, 165, 166
Kirkcaldy Property Investment Society 96
Kirkhill 133
Koch, Robert 15

L

labour, labourers 7, 14, 22-3, 39, 43, 46, 52, 55, 61, 64, 66, 80, 125, 128, 132, 138-9, 141, 146, 156
Lady Menzies Place 147, 159, 162
Lanarkshire 134-37, 164
land 27, 36, 38, 52-3, 63, 65, 74-5, 79, 83-5, 87-9, 92, 95, 100-1, 103, 111-12, 114, 116-18,

120, 132, 145-49
landlords 53, 99, 140, 148, 155
landowners 20, 27, 46, 87, 112, 147, 157
Laurel Terrace 103-4, 107, 160
Lauriston 95, 97
Lawnmarket 19
legislation 25, 36, 48
   City Improvement Act (1867) 133
   Conjugal Rights (Scotland) Act (1861) 143
   Edinburgh Municipality Extension Act (1856) 36
   Education Acts (1906, 1907) 123
   Housing Act (1919), (1923), and (1924) 124-25
   Industrial and Provident Societies Partnership Act (1852) 58
   Limited Liability Act (1855) 48
   Municipal Elections Amendment (Scotland) Act 1881, 143
   Rent Restrictions Act (1915) 123
Leith 60, 73, 81, 93, 108
Leith Wynd 55
Leven colony housing 151
Lewis Terrace 92, 159, 162
Lewis, David (councillor) 132
life expectancy 107,151
Lily Terrace 107
Littlejohn, Dr. Henry D. 14, 15, 29, 41, 63
Liverpool 22, 61
Lochend Road – see Restalrig 89, 91
lodging house 41-2, 53
London Road 25, 138, 151
Lothian Road 26

M

McLaren, Duncan 63, 132, 133
McLaren Terrace 132, 159, 162
McNaughton, Robert 102
marital status:
   married 7, 36, 63, 142-43, 145, 156-57, 166
   unmarried 143-45, 156-57, 167
   widow 7, 84, 115, 143-45, 157
   divorced 142-4
Maryfield 87, 88, 92, 93
Meadows 16, 21, 42, 96, 166
Menzies, Lady 87, 93, 147
Merchant Company 103, 107, 108, 114, 139, 144, 155
Methil 152
Metropolitan Association, housing 40
Miller, Hugh 56, 57, 166
Mill, George 110, 167
Mill, John Stuart *On Liberty* 58
'model' dwellings:
   Ashley Buildings 40, 48-9, 56
   Begg's Buildings 48-9, 51-2
   Blackwood's Buildings 48
   Chalmers Buildings 42-5, 48-50, 56
   Clermiston Buildings 48
   Croall's Buildings 48
   Gillis' Buildings 48
   Gladstone's Buildings 48
   Milne's Buildings 48, 50
   Patriot Hall 48, 50, 110, 168
   Pilrig Buildings 37-9, 42-3, 48-9, 56, 132
   Prince Albert Buildings 48
   Prospect Street 48
   Rae's Buildings 48
   Rosebank Cottages 44, 46-9, 51, 166
   Rosemount Buildings 46-50
   View Craig 48, 51
moral panic 55
mortality rates 16
Musselburgh 151
Musselburgh Building and Investment Society 96
mutuality principles 58-9, 61, 63, 66, 72, 97, 157
Myrtle Terrace 103-4, 160

N

Nasmith, David 21
New Town 20, 22, 27, 68, 88, 103, 155, 165
newspapers
   Edinburgh Courant 55, 86
   Edinburgh Weekly News 57, 167
   Scottish Press 57
   The Pilot 85
   The Scotsman 29, 42, 46, 55, 63, 64
   The Witness 55, 166
North British Railway 116
North British Rubber Company 105
North Fort Street 87
North Merchiston (Flowers) 33, 79, 102, 103, 104, 105, 107, 114, 132, 133, 137, 147
Norton Park 88, 132, 138, 140, 145

O

occupations 16, 22-23, 30, 39, 46, 59, 84-5, 106-7, 110, 138-41

Index

Old Town 13, 14, 19, 20, 22, 27, 49, 50, 53, 55, 72, 123, 133, 136, 138, 155, 164
overcrowding 13, 20, 29, 53

P

Palmerston, Lord 74, 75
philanthropy 50
Pilrig Model Buildings Association 38
Pitlochry Place 159
Pleasance 49, 72
Police Commissioners 16
Portsburgh 36
poverty 21, 29, 31, 32, 41, 53, 56, 151
population 13, 18-19, 21, 25, 27, 29, 31, 35-6, 56, 123, 135, 152
Portsburgh 36
Presbyterianism 20
Princes Street 41
Property Investment Company 83, 96, 103, 155
prostitution 56
public health 14, 16, 29, 35, 53, 56-7, 63, 107, 110-11, 123, 132, 140, 152

R

Reid, Sir Hugh Gilzean 10, 64, 131, 167
Restalrig 16, 79, 89, 91, 93, 99, 103, 110, 132, 135, 136, 138, 140, 145
Restalrig Park 87, 89, 94, 101, 112, 115, 116, 132, 134-35, 139, 142, 159, 162
Restalrig Road 94, 114
Rintoul Place 79, 93, 167
Rosebank Cottages 44, 46, 47, 80, 166
Rosemount Buildings 46, 47, 48, 50
Royal Colleges of Physicians and Surgeons 29, 31
Rutherglen 151, 152
Ryehill Terrace 114, 146

S

Salmond, Andrew (ECBC Chairman) 112, 126
Salmond Place 99, 159
Saughtonhall estate 116
Saughton Crescent 118
Saughtonhall Drive 116-19
Saxe Coburg Place 24, 25, 26, 68
schools 19, 23-4, 123, 129
  Broughton 123
  Edinburgh Ragged Schools 41
  Free Church 43, 48
  London Ragged School Union 41
  North Canongate 123
  Thornybauk 60
  Sunday 31
Scottish Industrial Museum 69
Scottish Metropolitan Property Company 155
Scottish National Exhibition 116, 118
Scottish Reformation Society 10
Social Reform Association 57
Scottish Property Investment Society 96, 103
Scottish Vulcanite Rubber Company 105
segregation 22-3
Selkirk 48, 129
Shaftesbury Park 110-20, 132-35, 137, 139, 147-48, 160-61
  Alderbank Terrace, Place, Gardens 114, 160, 163
  Almondbank Terrace 114, 160, 163
  Ashley Terrace 104, 107, 109, 114, 163
  Briarbank Terrace 114, 160, 163
  Hazelbank Terrace 113-14, 163
  Hollybank Terrace 111, 114, 160, 163
shares/shareholders 7, 11, 48, 70, 72, 73, 75, 79, 87, 88, 89, 101, 110, 112, 125, 126, 141, 155, 156, 169
Shaw Place 38-9, 43, 48
Silvermills 75, 155
Slateford Road 103, 106, 114
Smiles, Samuel *Self Help* 57
Spylaw House 129
Steel, James 87, 89, 147
Stockbridge 7, 10-11, 46, 71, 75-6, 79, 83-5, 87, 91-3, 99, 110, 114, 116, 118, 131-2, 135-6, 138-9, 145-6, 155, 159, 161, 165, 167
  Reid Terrace 7, 11, 25, 57, 69, 79, 84, 93, 131, 143, 159, 162
  Hugh Miller Place 57, 74, 79, 84, 93, 146, 159, 162
  Rintoul Place 79, 93, 111, 132, 156, 159, 162, 167
  Collins Place 93, 132, 159, 162, 167
  Colville Place 93, 159, 162
  Bell Place 93, 110, 159
  Kemp Place 93, 110, 159, 162, 165
  Glenogle Place, Terrace, House 69, 79, 93, 132, 159, 162
  Avondale Place 93, 159

Teviotdale Place 93, 159
  Balmoral, Dunrobin, Bridge Place 93, 159
Scot's Land 53
subsidies 125, 128, 148
Suburban Feuing Company 120, 155
suffrage 141

T

taxation, local valuation (Rates) 30, 36, 85, 124, 146, 148, 161
temperance 38, 51, 55-6, 131
tenants 7, 27, 30, 48, 52, 80, 83-5, 99, 112, 123, 140, 155
Tollcross 26, 95, 155, 168
Torphichen Street 69
Trades Council 60-1, 63
trade associations 72
trade unions 63

Trafalgar Street 81, 85, 86, 111
Trinity Hospital 87

V

Victoria Lodging House 41, 42
Violet Terrace 104, 105

W

Walker, James 46, 50, 87, 89, 147
Walker Terrace 93
war 7, 33, 51, 118, 123, 125-28
water 14-15, 29, 39, 41, 44, 49, 53, 74-5, 83, 153
water closet (WC) 15, 44, 49, 53
Water Lane 9, 69, 75
Water of Leith 49, 61, 75, 116, 117

Waverley Temperance Hotel 51
West Port 49, 55, 123
women
  household heads 7, 49, 141-45
  divorce rates 142-43
  home ownership 7
  lodgers 42
  marital status 143-44, 156-57, 167
  National Society for Women's Suffrage (1867) 141, 143
  occupations 16
  relief 21
  rentier incomes 96, 106, 157
  shareholders (ECBC) 70, 141, 156
  voting rights 143, 151, 157
Women's Liberal Association 57

Richard Rodger, MA., PhD has published over 100 journal articles and books on his wide-ranging research interests on the economic and social history of towns and cities since 1750. Titles include *Scottish Housing in the 20th Century; Housing in Urban Britain 1780-1914;* the prize-winning book: *The Transformation of Edinburgh: Land, Property and Trust in the 19th Century*; and *Insanitary City: H. D. Littlejohn and the Condition of Edinburgh* (with Paul Laxton) which received widespread acclaim for its scholarship, production standards, and penetrating insights into the links between poverty, employment and public health in Victorian cities. Rodger's texts for the series of Student Guides entitled *Software Made Simple* gained many plaudits, and the Plain English Society's Crystal Mark – for plain English!

He has held academic posts at Liverpool, Leicester and Kansas Universities and also had a number of visiting academic positions. He was Editor of the journal *Urban History* for many years, and General Editor of 37 books in the Series 'Historical Urban Studies'. He is a Fellow of the Academy of Social Sciences and Emeritus Professor of Economic and Social History at the University of Edinburgh.